The Mainspring of Economic Development

PRIYATOSH MAITRA

ST. MARTIN'S PRESS   NEW YORK

Library of Congress Cataloging in Publication Data

Maitra, Priyatosh.
    The mainspring of economic development.

    Includes bibliographical references and index.
        1. Industrialization.   2. Economic development.
3. Underdeveloped areas.   I. Title.
HD2326.M23 1980   338.9   79-21657
ISBN 0-312-50453-5

CONTENTS

PREFACE

This book has grown out of two papers, one presented at the International Symposium on the Problems of Take-Off held at the L'Bocconi University, Milan in June 1976 and the other at the Seventh International Economic History Congress, Edinburgh, August 1978. This book deals with the basic force behind the Industrial Revolution of the nineteenth and twentieth centuries on the one hand, and the basic characteristics of both successful and unsuccessful cases of imported industrialisation on the other. I have made a particular attempt to study the effects of population pressure on agrarian technology and the organisation of production, and technology transfer as a means to achieve economic development. Cases of unsuccessful imported industrialisation (i.e. the cases of the Third World countries) are analysed, as are the views of Marx and Marxists on the introduction of Western capital to underdeveloped countries.

My research has revealed basic faults in the current approaches toward development pursued in underdeveloped countries.

I owe much to the University of Otago for providing me with research facilities and a rewarding intellectual climate within which this work became possible.

I am especially in the debt of Michael Cooper, Chairman, Department of Economics at this University who read the manuscript of this book and saved me from many errors of omission and commission and contributed towards the improvement of its contents. Any remaining errors, however, are mine. I am grateful to John Child of Economic History for ungrudging advice and help in pursuing this research. Alan Maynard of York University, Peter Henderson and Mark Olssen of this University have also helped me over many hurdles at various stages in this work.

To John Omer-Cooper, Ron Lister and Richard Kamman of of this University, and Ajit K. Dasgupta of Delhi University, I owe further enormous debt for their views and comments, all of which helped me a great deal in the early formulation of my ideas.

I am also indebted to participants at the International Symposium, Milan (1976) and the Seventh International Economic History Congress, Edinburgh (1978) and in particular I. Gasparini of L'Bocconi University, Milan, Paul Bairoch of the University of Geneva and N. Hatti of the University of Lund, Sweden for helpful comments on my two papers which foreshadowed the main theme of this book.

To Ruth Harper go my particular thanks for her ungrudging help in organising and typing the materials for this book.

I am indebted to my wife, Romola, and daughters, Rupa and Nipa, for encouragement and for providing an environment conducive for the writing of this book.

Priyatosh Maitra
Department of Economics
University of Otago

1 INTRODUCTION

All industrial 'latecomers', i.e. underdeveloped countries of the present century, are trying to develop their economies through industrialisation without an industrial revolution. These countries are following examples of industrialisation from the late nineteenth and early twentieth centuries, in countries successful in industrialisation without an industrial revolution (e.g. India and other underdeveloped countries). This process is being helped by unlimited supplies of capital, skill and technology from pioneer industrial countries. Economic theories of development emphasise the advantages of being latecomers because this type of industrialisation does not result in social disruption and the waste of resources in trial and error, and, instead, helps to achieve rapid industrial growth.

Elsewhere, I have attempted to analyse what this has actually meant in terms of the development of the industrial latecomer countries of this century.[1] Here, I have first tried to point out basic patterns of economic development with or without an industrial revolution in the nineteenth and twentieth centuries (shown in Tables 1.1 and 1.2), and then important factors responsible for the failure of the underdeveloped countries of today to industrialise despite the fact that modern industries (e.g. textiles, railways, plantations, mining etc.) were introduced long ago in these countries, in some cases more than a hundred years ago (e.g. India). I will also discuss the patterns of the industrial revolution of the twentieth century. I have added a section on the meaning and significance of the classical Industrial Revolution that took place in the eighteenth century in the UK. No attempt has been made to re-define the Industrial Revolution. The accepted concept has been used. I will also take a brief look at the process of imported industrialisation that characterised the French, German and Japanese development. I will draw extensively from authorities such as Cipolla (1973),[2] Bairoch (1973),[3] Henderson (1954),[4] Hohenberg (1972),[5] Hobsbawm (1969),[6] Hisao Otsuka (1965),[7] Landes (1965),[8] Clough and Rapp (1970)[9] and Tranter (1973)[10] to make my point in this connection.

The industrial revolution, as they conceive it, is first and foremost an agricultural revolution for the obvious reason that agriculture in the pre-industrial period was the main centre of social, political and cultural activities and the main source of a living to ninety per cent of the total

Table 1.1:   Industrialisation with Industrial Revolution

	Basic Features			

1. 19th Century

(1)	(2)	(3)	(4)	(5)
Fundamental changes in Agrarian Economic Structure and other economic organisations occurred spontaneously. Agriculture, being the dominating sector absorbed more than 90 per cent of the country's resources. Industrial Revolution started from agriculture.	No dualistic structure evolved for obvious reasons	It took place in the framework of perfectly competitive capitalism	Growth of indigenous technology	Initial rate of growth is not remarkable

2. 20th Century

(1)	(2)	(3)	(4)	(5)
Fundamental changes in socio-economic organisation and production relations brought about by conscious social decision	No dualism for obvious reasons	It takes place in the framework of socialist ownership of means of production, economic resources and wealth	Growth of indigenous technology	Very high rate of growth

Table 1.2:   Industrialisation without Industrial Revolution[1]

	Basic Features			

1. 19th Century

(1)	(2)	(3)	(4)	(5)
Very little change in the agrarian economic structure. In fact, Industrialisation was not a product of the needs of agriculture, although it was the dominating sector. Industrialisation was merely a case of transplantation from the UK	Dualism became inevitable at the initial stage of development. Existence of large external markets helped rapid growth and integration[2]	It took place in the framework of monopoly capitalism[3]	Primarily based on imported capital and technology— little growth of indigenous technology. It is an imposition from the top, and helped and protected by the state	Very high rate of growth

2. 20th Century: (a) Same as above in the case of successful industrialisation
                 (b) For unsuccessful ones (i.e. underdeveloped countries) the
                     story is different in the sense that these basic features are
                     clearly evident for these economies, but without the success
                     in development.

Notes: 1. In the case of newly settled countries i.e. USA, Canada, Australia and
New Zealand, dualism still persists in the form of underdeveloped economies of
American Indians and Eskimos of North America, Aborigines in Australia and
Maoris in New Zealand. Those underdeveloped regions within the highly developed
countries are called today the Fourth World. This aspect has been discussed in the
text.
2. Discussed in the text.
3. 'The formation of trusts, syndicates and so on became the characteristics of
Germany and U.S.A. in the 1880s.' Chs. 9 and 10, *Industry and Empire*, Hobsbawm,
E.J., Pelican, London, 1969. In the Japanese economy the role of Zaibatsu is well
known today. That monopolies dominate the modern sector of underdeveloped
economies does not need any elaboration. There are two important reasons: (i)
imported industrialisation needs relatively large resources, mobilisation of which
is in most cases beyond the ability of small-scale proprietary firms. This task becomes
feasible when firms are organised into larger corporate monopolistic ones integrated
with financial institutions; (ii) as imported capital and technology are relatively
more productive and capital intensive, the economies of scale of production requiring larger market make classical perfect competition most uneconomical and un-
workable, particularly in poor income economies. Small scale economic activities
based on simple technology can survive in an atmosphere of perfect competition.
Capital intensive large-scale organisation in a private enterprise economic system
needs monopolistic-oligopolistic market conditions mainly for above reasons
among others.

Source: from the author's paper presented at the International Symposium,
L'Bocconi University, Milan, June 1976—to be published.

population. Naturally, in a society where an industrial revolution
occurred, it started in the reorganisation of the agrarian economy, the
dominant sector of the time, which released resources to permit and
foster an unprecedented development not only of the industrial and
service sectors but also of the social, scientific and cultural life. An
industrial revolution is above all a socio-cultural phenomenon.[11] This
is true of the Soviet industrial revolution of 1917 and the Chinese one
of the 1950s. These are discussed in detail in the sections on Russia
and China in this book. Hobsbawm wrote: 'The Industrial Revolution
does not merely mean an acceleration of economic growth but an acceleration of growth because of and through economic transformation'.[12]

From a narrow technological and economic point of view, the
industrial revolution is regarded as the process by which a society gains
control of vast sources of energy and thereby experiences accelerated
economic growth; but such a definition has serious limitations as it does

not do justice to this phenomenon either as regards the distinct origin of the phenomenon itself, or as regards its cultural, economic, social and political implications. Also it does not deal with the phenomenon of the growth of technology and industries in economies where agriculture and large human resources remain underdeveloped; in other words it does not make any distinction between cases of industrial revolution and of imported industrialisation.

The Industrial Revolution in the late eighteenth century in England brought about a jump in the course of history but unlike the attempted industrialisation process of the mid-twentieth century, it was rooted in the past. Cipolla wrote: 'In order to discover the origins of the Industrial Revolution, one must go back to that profound change in ideas and social structure that accompanied the rise of urban communes preceding such changes. To understand the essential significance of the rise of these urban centres and their new culture, one must emphasise its revolutionary character, the revolt against the predominant agrarian-feudal order.'[13]

I wish to emphasise here that the present urban centres in underdeveloped countries have not evolved in the way described above. These centres were not products of the evolution of the indigenous society. They were built up to meet the needs of colonial powers or of foreign investors who came from industrialised countries. Take for example the case of Calcutta which was built up from three villages to meet, first, the needs of the East India Company and then the British industrial economy. The indigenous urban centres of the time (e.g. Murshidabad or Dacca) which had evolved historically as rich, urban centres were by-passed for economic reasons. But such reasons could not be the reasons of the indigenous economy and society because of completely different historical and factor-endowment situations. Consequently urban centres isolated from any historical base were established and the old natural centres did not evolve into industrial urban centres and in course of time, died out. This is only one way but an important one, to look at the phenomenon. But we can also look at it as a development from the angle of economic causation. In this respect, we must examine the causation of the industrial revolution in terms of changes in population growth and its impact on existing resources, necessitating changes in technology and, consequently, economic organisation.

Notes

1. P. Maitra, *Underdevelopment Revisited* (Firma KLM, Calcutta, 1977), Ch. 2.

2. C.M. Cipolla (ed.), *The Industrial Revolution* (Fontana, London, 1973).

3. P. Bairoch, 'Agriculture and the Industrial Revolution 1700-1914' in Cipolla, pp. 488-92.

4. W.O. Henderson, *Britain and Industrial Europe 1750-1870* (Liverpool University Press, 1954).

5. P. Hohenberg, 'Changes in Rural France in the Period of Industrialisation', *Journal of Economic History*, vol. 32, no. 1 (March 1972).

6. E.J. Hobsbawm, *Industry and Empire* (Pelican, Harmondsworth, 1969), Chs. 2 and 10.

7. H. Otsuka, 'Modernisation Re-considered with special reference to Japan', *The Developing Economies*, vol. 3, no. 4 (December 1965).

8. D.S. Landes, 'Japan and Europe' in W. Lockwood (ed.), *The State and Economic Enterprise in Japan* (Princeton University Press, 1965).

9. S.B. Clough and R.T. Rapp, *European Economic History* (McGraw Hill, 1975).

10. N. Tranter, *Population Since the Industrial Revolution* (Croom Helm, London, 1973).

11. Cipolla, *Industrial Revolution*, p. 12.

12. Hobsbawm, *Industry*, p. 34.

13. Cipolla, *Industrial Revolution*, p. 9.

2 THE INDUSTRIAL REVOLUTION

(I) The Concept and the Process

Modern economic development was initiated by the industrial revolution of the late eighteenth century – which was the culmination of the process of agricultural change of the previous century. The agricultural revolution followed from the pressure of an increasing population on existing modes of production and on resources, which led to the changes in agricultural technology that in turn necessitated changes in the agrarian organisation and production relationships of the time, so that more resources could be made available to give effect to technological changes. (This point is discussed in detail later.) This entire process evolved into the industrial revolution which was accompanied by socio-political reorganisation. The pressure of population on the existing resources necessitated increased output and since at that time more than 80 per cent of the total population depended on agriculture, the pressure of population was most felt in that sector. Thus all industrial revolutions must have their roots in agriculture. This is equally true of the twentieth-century cases of industrial revolution, e.g. the Soviet industrial revolution since the 1920s and the Chinese one since the 1950s.

On the other hand, there are cases of nineteenth-century imported industrialisation (the process of industrialisation owing its origin to the classic Industrial Revolution of England) which have all the characteristics of an industrial revolution, except that they were not initiated to meet the needs of the agricultural sector. Neither did they result from the increased productivity of agriculture; the industrialisation was transplanted from England to the urban sectors of these economies to fulfil the needs of a handful of the mercantile class. Pressure of population led to institutional changes, abolition of serfdom, land reforms and political changes (e.g. the French Revolution of 1789, the German revolution of 1848 and the Meiji Restoration of 1868 in Japan) and also piecemeal changes in the technology of agriculture. But these changes in agriculture did not initiate the growth of modern industries. (For detailed discussion see section on Germany, France and Japan.) Industries were essentially based on technology, capital and skills imported from England. We have used the cases of France, Germany and Japan as examples of this type of development. These are, no doubt, successful cases of industrialisation without an industrial revolution. There are also cases of imported industrialisation in the twentieth century which are without exception unsuccessful in reaching take-off stage to self-sustained growth.

In the case of underdeveloped countries today, the process of industrialisation has not evolved out of agriculture despite the fact that nearly 80 per cent of the total population depends on agriculture for its living. The pressure of population has failed to spur agricultural innovation leading to an industrial revolution. Industrialisation is already there, implanted from outside, but it has little to do with utilisation of domestic human resources. Thus in this process the human resources of these countries are left unutilised or underutilised.

The industrial revolution is the rise of modern industry, not the rise of industry as such.[1] Many parts of Europe became increasingly industrialised in the sense that a growing proportion of their labour potential was allocated to industry.[2] (The same is true of many parts of Asia.) But the type of industry that characterised these industrial activities of the pre-industrial revolution days—the traditionally organised, family-labour-based rural handicrafts—hardly has the appearance of a modern economy that owes its origin to an industrial revolution. The industrial revolution is thus different from the case of the development of proto-industrial activities in the sense that the former reflect the socio-economic changes initiated by the increasing pressure of population that necessitates changes in the technology used in the proto-industrialisation period.

Pressure of population necessitated changes in methods, practices and techniques in agricultural production which in turn necessitated changes in agrarian organisation. This must be distinguished from what is happening today in underdeveloped countries. Undoubtedly these economies are facing an unprecedented growth of population, although the forces behind it are fundamentally different from those behind the growth in the pre-industrial revolution days in England (see Chapter 3). One basic difference between the two situations is that in developed countries the growth of population in the eighteenth and nineteenth centuries may be termed as 'population take-off' whereas that in twentieth-century Third World countries is 'population inflation'.[3] To achieve growth in output to feed this growing population, technology and capital are being transferred from an environment ('environment' here is defined in terms of factor-endowment situation, economic needs etc., resulting from a different historical process of development, and is considered as the determining factor of the development of technology and capital) which is completely different from that of the underdeveloped countries and as a consequence the huge transfer of technology and capital in recent times has caused an unprecedented rate of growth in output but failed to stimulate demand for human resources. Professor Jones wrote that the significance of the development in the methods of farm production at the time of the industrial revolution of the eighteenth century was that they were yeast trying to ferment a rather cold agrarian structure. They came first because they represented the most sharply changing element within agriculture and the one which contributed most obviously to rising production during this period (i.e. 1650-1815). 'The matrix of tenurial arrangements, farm-size distribution and field lay-out within which they acted did alter considerably in favour of large-scale production for the market, but comparatively slowly. The organisational evolution formed a century-old continuum in England, so did technical advances, but as decisive an upturn as can ever be detected in rate of agricultural change occurred in their case in the mid-seventeenth century.'[4]

Population growth which was varying from minus to plus 0.5 per cent per annum in the pre-industrial days did bring about some improvements in food production, and other non-agricultural activities which were being undertaken in traditional ways.

Arnold Toynbee wrote of the 1730s that improvements had been made in sheep breeds by changing rams and by sowing turnips and grass seed, and there was high quality wool to be found in most counties in England.[5]

E.L. Jones wrote: 'The middle of the seventeenth century seems the most appropriate starting point for the infinitely expandable improvements of farming practice . . . The crucial innovations pertained to the supply of fodder, partly in the diffusion of the turnip as field crop but more important at that early date the first widespread cultivation of clover, sanfoin and ryegrass, with the vigorous "floating" of water meadows i.e. the irrigation of streamside pasture. These crops and practices with later additions like the swede (a much hardier root) went on spreading into new counties, new estates, new farms and new fields throughout this period.'[6]

This gradual development was inspired by a change in the ratio of cereal to livestock prices in favour of expanding livestock production from approximately the mid-seventeenth to mid-eighteenth century. Jones comments: 'By the second half of the eighteenth century where there was renewed pressure on cereal production, there was no danger of a recession of forage crops—mixed farming had come to stay, since its fat stock or its cereal enterprises offered reasonable returns under most market conditions. Often both paid well.'[7]

But population growth rate showed a consistent upturn of one per cent per annum from the 1760s until the 1840s, and after that at 1.8 per cent until the first decade of the twentieth century. This consistent increase in population accompanied by the increasing ability to improve modes of production acted as a great stimulus for further development. In the beginning of this period, because of the low level of technology, growing population was considered as the greatest asset in terms of labour and energy required for increasing output. With the development of technology based on science in the subsequent period that resulted from the improvement of skills, knowledge, organisation and efficiency, the quantity of labour began to be increasingly replaced in importance by the quality of labour in order to meet the challenge of the expanding markets of the pioneer industrial countries with declining population growth rates. The rate of growth of capital formation and of product- ivity soon far exceeded the rate of growth of the labour force. But, as pointed out above, this situation contrasts with that at the beginning of the industrial revolution. In the period between 1760 and 1840 the pop- ulation growth rate was high, at one per cent per annum, which could be considered both as a stimulating force behind the rapid agricultural change leading to the Industrial Revolution, and as itself a product of such development. In other words, changes in the modes and organ- isation of production (e.g. enclosures and changes in crop practices, i.e. wheat cultivation replacing barley etc.) meant more labour was needed because of the low level of technology and capital and this in turn stim- ulated fertility. This is a lesson that underdeveloped countries should learn from the experience of the Industrial Revolution.

According to Paul Bairoch's study,[8] on the eve of the industrial rev- olution, at the beginning of the eighteenth century, the most highly developed societies still had to keep 75 to 80 per cent of their labour force employed in agriculture. At the same time the average consumption of food products was not only low in terms of calories (see Table 2.1 which shows little difference in the level of calorie consumption between England in the pre-industrial revolution days and underdeveloped countries today) but also consisted almost entirely of calories of vegetable origin. Consumption of calories of animal origin was very low because they were costly; at that time it took eight vegetable calories to produce one animal calory. Thus in traditional societies the average agricultural worker produced an amount of food only about 20 to 30 per cent in excess of his family's consumption. This 20 to 30 per cent surplus acquires special meaning if we take into account a factor often omitted from theories of

Table 2.1:   Net Food Consumption in Developing Countries: Calorie Intake (A daily consumption of 2,500 calories per head in England in 1750 may be compared to these figures.[1])

	Country	Period	Daily Consumption of Calories, *per capita*
Below 2000	Bolivia	1964-6	1760
	India	1969-70	1990
	Indonesia	1970	1920
	Tanzania	1970	1700
2000-2400	Afghanistan	1964-6	2060
	Burma	1964-6	2010
	Ceylon	1970	2340
	China	1966	2100-2200
	Columbia	1970	2140
	Iran	1964-6	2030
	Iraq	1964-6	2050
	Jamaica	1964-6	2280
	Kenya	1970	2200
	W. Malaysia	1970	2190
	Nigeria	1970	2290
	Peru	1968	2190
	Thailand	1964-6	2210
	Tunisia	1964-6	2200
	Zambia	1964-6	2250
2400 and above	Brazil	1970	2820
	Chile	1970	2560
	Cuba	1964-6	2500
	Egypt	1968-9	2770
	Israel	1969-70	2990
	Jordan	1964-6	2400
	Republic of Korea	1969	2490
	Malawi	1970	2400
	Mexico	1964-6	2620
	Mongolia	1964-6	2540
	Pakistan	1969-70	2410
	Paraguay	1970	2540
	Syria	1964-6	2450
	Turkey	1964-6	2760
	Venezuela	1970	2430

Note: 1. It is important to note here that calorie requirements vary with age, body weight and stature, and climatic conditions, and because of them . . . 'the calorie needs of the people in the less developed regions are smaller than those of the people in Europe and N. America'. (F.A.O., Third World *Food Survey*, Rome, 1963, p. 37).
Sources: FAO *Production Year Book* (1971), Table 136 and Deleyne (1973), p. 56.

economic development, namely, the yearly fluctuations of agricultural yields, which even at a national level could amount to an average of over 25 per cent. In consequence, periodical subsistence crises became inevitable which, at their worst, could produce a decline in economic life and hence in the civilisation it supported. For this reason, as long as agricultural productivity had not progressed beyond this stage, it is practically impossible to conceive of a continuous progress in the development of civilisation, let alone of the acceleration of scientific and technical progress, that is an essential characteristic of modern times. At this level of development, a sustained growth of population accompanied by changes in agrarian organisation and crop practices alone could ensure sustained increase in agricultural productivity.

In England, agricultural development resulting from the increasing pressure of population stimulated an increased demand for consumer goods and especially for textile products, thus providing an important stimulus towards the launching of the industrial revolution. According to Paul Bairoch, 'agriculture played a major part in the birth of the modern iron and steel industry in England without which all the technical advances that characterised the industrial revolution would have been made impossible'.[9] A brief account of the interrelationship between the development of agriculture and the birth of the modern iron and steel industry will help us in understanding the process of the industrial revolution in England. The widespread mechanisation of agriculture took a long time because of the availability of cheap labour and alternative simple technology. New and better implements made of iron and steel began to be used increasingly to make labour more productive. In Britain, the agricultural labour force grew by 24 per cent between 1800 and 1850 while the demand for crops increased by more than 50 per cent. This increase in demand for food may be explained by two factors: (i) the demand of the increasing urban population and (ii) relatively high-income elasticity of demand for food. This increase in crop output was made possible by the use of better implements made of iron and by changes in agricultural organisation.

This account is not applicable to cases of industrialisation without an industrial revolution. We will discuss later other distinctive features, such as the differences in population growth, land-plot size, and changes in technology between the two processes of development. We will base our discussion of the iron and steel industry mainly on Bairoch's works.[10]

From 1700 onwards there was an unprecedented growth of population in Europe i.e. from an estimated 100 to 220 million in 1700 to 1,900 million in 1800. In England the population growth rate was high and steady at about one per cent until 1850 and then 1.8 per cent until 1910. Malthus, alarmed by this rapid growth in the population, wrote his first essay on population in 1798. The early growth rate of population at one per cent was high when it is considered in the context of the prevailing technology and organisation. This high population growth rate brought about changes in technology necessitating changes in economic organisation. These in turn stimulated fertility and changes in technology made possible increased supply of food, better housing, improved sanitation etc., causing a decline in the death rate, together resulting in a high population growth rate known as the 'population revolution'.[11] At the same time demand for labour was high in the main urban industries; in the rural areas, the enclosure movement, instead of releasing the labour force to urban areas, initially meant that more of the human resources released by changes in economic organisation were needed. In other words, the technological change that was taking place was labour intensive and led to increased demand for labour in both sectors.

The rural sector—employing some 75 to 80 per cent of the working population—initiated the agricultural revolution towards the beginning of the eighteenth century. The agrarian innovations connected with that revolution had a direct impact on iron consumption and consequently had the effect of making more productive use of growing population, for example, in the form of the gradual elimination of fallow land clearance and improvement of neglected land, improved equipment, new types of implements, and the wider use of horses and horse-shoeing.[12] All these improvements needed more labour, the mode of production being simple and labour-intensive. These changes meant a reorganisation of the agrarian structure in the form of enclosures, which, contrary to popular belief, required an increase in the labour force. In practice it can be estimated that at the outset of the agricultural revolution some 45 per cent of available land was given up to fallow, while 50 to 60 years later that proportion fell to 20 per cent, which would imply an increase of 45 per cent in ploughing and related farm work.[13] This in turn meant a greater use of implements and a proportionate increase in iron consumption—resulting in more productive use of labour and other resources. These developments needed, as the condition of their success, the basic changes in agrarian organisation that were heralded by the enclosures. Similarly, in the twentieth-century cases of industrial revolution (e.g. USSR and China), the more productive use of resources for achieving a higher level of development required fundamental changes in the agrarian organisation. However, these changes were different in the two cases – the former resulting spontaneously from individual initiative and the latter from a socially conscious attempt due to different historical conditions.

Available sources suggest that in England output per worker in agriculture rose by about 100 per cent between 1700 and 1800. In a society where some 65 to 70 per cent of the working population was engaged in agriculture, such an advance in agricultural productivity had a wide impact. At this time labour-saving mechanical devices were not available, but improved implements like sickles, hoes and scythes made of iron were in wide use. Improvements in agricultural implements gradually led to the replacement of the wooden plough by iron ones. The Rotherham plough (1730) incorporated much more iron in its construction than the traditional plough, and the wider use of horses for farm work and the practice of shoeing them were also very significant in their effect on the demand for iron. For example, some estimates of the impact on the demand for iron of shoeing farm horses, calculated on the basis of the number of horses at work and the average use of iron involved in their shoeing, suggest that the demand thus created represented about 15 per cent of total iron consumption in England in 1760.[14]

Thus, the combined effect of these various factors (i.e. changes in crop practices, improvement of implements and changes in the organisation of agriculture etc.) resulted in a great increase in agriculture's demand for iron, but also in its demand for labour. Therefore the improvement in technology and organisation in agriculture did not release sufficient labour for the industrial sector. At the same time, the agricultural revolution provided farmers with the economic means to acquire all this new equipment through the increased yields they secured by the change in methods. The demand for iron from agricultural sources at this time was very high. Excluding the farmers' private consumption, it can be estimated at between 30 to 50 per cent of the total demand for iron. The constantly rising demand from agriculture produced strong pressure on the iron industry. In England this demand provided a powerful stimulus towards eliminating the main bottleneck in the domestic iron industry – the shortage of fuel, specifically wood. This was how, as a result of the increased demand from agriculture, the major technical innovation in the iron industry came to be introduced – namely, the use of coal instead of wood as the basic combustible for blast-furnaces; it spread rapidly, opening the way for the numerous technical inventions that made the industrial revolution possible. For, though the economic role of the iron industry was not as important as that of cotton in the early stages of that revolution, iron nevertheless played a major and decisive part in carrying out technical innovations in all spheres of activity. Without supplies of low-cost iron it would have been impossible to extend widely the use of machines in which iron played an important part. And it was because of the greater use of iron that more productive machines could be built.[15] Thus, the agricultural revolution which in essence takes the form of an agrarian reorganisation, contributed decisively to industrialisation by promoting changes in a vital part of mechanisation.

The profound changes in the system of agricultural production that preceded the technological revolution reduced the risk of famine, and thus provoked the consequent changes in socio-economic and political organisation, the sum total of which may be termed the industrial revolution. 'The resultant increase in productivity led in the space of 40 to 60 years to the transition from all average surplus of the order of 25 percent to something more like 50 percent or more, thus surpassing — for the first time in the history of mankind — what might be called the risk of famine limit; the agricultural revolution — for so these profound changes in rural life have been rightly called — ended the deadlock, thus prepared the way for the industrial revolution.'[16] In countries where industrial development came late the demand created by railway construction was the basis for a modern iron and steel industry. 'This was not the case, however, in England, the birth place of the industrial revolution. It could have been otherwise, for railways were the outcome of the gradual development of the steam engine which had itself been fostered by the growing needs of industrialisation imported from the birth place in the industrial revolution.'

Another important fact is that, in the first stages, the main body of capital and more particularly of entrepreneurs that produced the upheavals of the industrial revolution was of modest proportions and always of agricultural origin. (This is, however, not applicable to industrial latecomers.) Technology was simple and labour-intensive. A more important change was in the form of organisation. The agricultural revolution in England was marked by the gradual elimination of fallow land and its replacement by the continuous rotation of crops and the introduction of new crops e.g. turnips, clover, maize, carrots, cabbages and lastly potatoes. Obviously, these changes in crop practices stimulated the improve-

ment of traditional farm implements and the introduction of new
implements in the form of the iron plough, and the use of iron in making other agricultural implements as noted earlier. They also encouraged
innovations such as the scythe, which gradually replaced the sickle, and
the mower, and led to the replacement of broadcast sowing and other
old methods. These changes were meant to improve the productivity of
agricultural labour and land.

The machine era was still to come when industrialisation advanced
and created a further increase in demand for labour. The extension of
the use of horses for farm work which created further demand for iron,
and the extension and improvement of arable land marked the profound
changes in agricultural modes of production. These changes created the
conditions for a reorganisation of land ownership and the size of holdings
which in turn furthered the introduction of agricultural techniques leading to the industrial revolution.

At the initial stage of the industrial revolution, machines and techniques of production were simple and required more labour.

Changes in agricultural tools that took place in the mid-nineteenth
century may be noted here briefly. Technological change, when it appeared, first took the form not of mechanisation but of a switch from lower
into higher working-capacity hand tools. Thus, as an intermediate step
the heavy hook, or more often the scythe, superceded the traditional
toothed sickle and smooth reap hook as the standard corn-harvesting
tools, first for the spring grains, barley and oats and then for the bread
grains, wheat and rye.

Mechanisation of production process in agriculture took a long time
as the technology at that time was simple and therefore these changes
absorbed labour. However, changes in technology were faster than elsewhere for reasons stated earlier.

As E.J.T. Collins wrote, 'the reaping machines gained ground faster
in Britain than elsewhere in Europe because of the higher average size
of farms and an earlier decline of the harvest work force. Even so, less
than 30 percent of the British harvest was mechanised in 1871'.[17]

The following extract from Hobsbawm's work *Industry and Empire*
may be used as a support to the above:

> The technological problems of the early Industrial Revolution were
> fairly simple. They required no class of men with specialised scien-
> tific qualifications, but merely a sufficiency of men with ordinary
> literacy familiar with simple mechanical devices and the working of
> metals, practical experience and initiative. The centuries since 1500

had certainly provided such a supply. Most of the new technical inventions and productive establishments could be started economically on a small scale and expanded piecemeal by successive addition. That is to say, they required little initial investment, and their expansion could be financed out of accumulated profits. Industrial development was only within the capacity of a multiplicity of small entrepreneurs and skilled traditional artisans. No twentieth century country setting about industrialisation has, or can have, anything like these advantages.[18]

Hobsbawm's conclusion is not based on historical analysis of the latter countries in the sense that any account of economic activities in most of these underdeveloped countries, particularly of India in the eighteenth and nineteenth centuries, would show that these economies also had skilled traditional artisan classes and entrepreneurs and rich cottage and small-scale industries (for a detailed discussion see Chapter 3). But the growth of population and its pressure on resources were not enough to lead to the kind of industrial change that took place in England at the comparable period. And then came the impact of technology transfer from the West, the consequences of which are discussed later. (See Chapter 3.)

The simple level of technology of the early nineteenth century could be assessed from the following account given by Knowles. He quoted from Smiles' Industrial Biography:

The early machine makers were men in quite a small way, and had been as a rule apprenticed to blacksmiths, carpenters or millwrights. Machines were all made by hand, every screw varied and every bolt and nut was of a sort special to itself. As everything depended on the dexterity of hand and correctness of eye of the workmen the work turned out was of very unequal merit besides being exceedingly costly. Even in the construction of comparatively simple machines the expense was so great as to present a formidable obstacle to their introduction and extensive use.

When once the machine was set up there was no guarantee that it would work properly, so inaccurate and faulty was it in its parts.

Not fifty years since [says Smiles, writing in 1863] it was the matter of the utmost difficulty to get an engine to work and sometimes of equal difficulty to keep it going. Though fitted by competent observers it often would not go at all. Then the foreman of the factory at which it was made was sent for and he would almost live beside the machine for a month or more; and after easing her here and screwing her up there, putting in a new part and altering an old one, packing the piston and tightening the valves the machine would at length be got to work.[19]

All this points to the important fact that the entire process needed more labour and used it more productively.

Sir William Fairbairn, as quoted in Knowles, stated that when he came to Manchester in 1814 'with the exception of very imperfect lathes and a few drills the whole of the machinery was executed by hand'.

Great Britain had to evolve engineering and create and train a race of engineers before she could carry out a radical transformation of her industrial methods. In the process she trained engineers nor merely for herself but for all Europe. According to *Reports on the Export of Machinery* (1824, 1825 and 1841), when England developed after 1820 the tools for making machines, the Continent was said to have gained an enormous advantage in making machinery for itself as then a lower degree of skill in the artisan was required.[20]

The tendency of factories to use steam is especially noticeable after 1815. The employment of steam as power meant that the machinery became larger and more powerful and the machines were no longer suitable for young children.[21] (The demographic impacts will be discussed in Chapter 3.)

Mechanical production provided more and not less employment, steadier work and better pay. The British artisan became unrivalled as a skilled worker and helped to train Europe. W.O. Henderson's account of Britain's contribution to the industrialisation of the Continent is also an important testimony to this.

I will discuss some aspects of the enclosure as far as is relevant for the main theme of this book before I proceed to examine cases of imported industrialisation in France, Germany and Japan.

(II) Population and Changes in Agrarian Organisation

Population growth created a pressure on existing resources and technology leading to innovation in agriculture and increases in income, and these became the basis for larger families and population growth.

In the case of England, the country of classical industrial revolution, we see from Table 2.2 how the balance between population and agri-

Table 2.2: Population and Agricultural Output in England and Wales, 1700-1829

Decade	Population (in millions)	Output of Grain (in millions of quarters)	Output *per capita*
1700-9	5.8	17.8	2.55
1710-19	6.0	15.4	2.57
1720-9	6.0	15.6	2.60
1730-9	5.9	15.3	2.59
1740-9	5.9	15.4	2.61
1750-9	6.1	16.5	2.70
1760-9	6.6	17.0	2.58
1770-9	7.1	17.4	2.45
1780-9	7.5	18.6	2.48
1790-9	8.3	19.9	2.39
1800-9	9.0	21.1	2.34
1810-19	10.3	24.4	2.37
1820-9	12.1	27.9	2.31

Source: Phyllis Deane and W.A. Cole, *British Economic Growth, 1688-1959* (1969), based on Tables 17 and 23.

cultural output was maintained as both spiralled upwards. The accelerated population growth was due partly to diminishing mortality rates, partly to the first incidence of 'demographic transition' in a period of rising income and partly to the stimulus given to fertility as a result of the increased demand for labour in both urban and rural areas.

From the table, it may be noted that the growth of grain production was smoother over the eighteenth century than was population growth. The latter was slow around about the 1780s and then increased dramatically.

The English case represents the basic relationship between population growth (as a source of both labour supply and final demand), and the growth of output, in an industrial revolution. The various aspects of this process will be discussed in more detail in subsequent sections.

Economic historians have been inclined to portray the coming of the new agriculture as something sudden and as a necessary precursor of the Industrial Revolution. According to recent studies, however, the eighteenth-century agricultural change known as the 'agricultural revolution' had very long antecedents.

But the most important feature that marked the eighteenth-century agricultural revolution was the change in agrarian organisation and production relations. The changes in agricultural methods in pre-industrial days may be summed up as follows. Since the middle ages advances had been going on in European agriculture: the introduction of the horse collar, and of horse-drawn implements, similar to the cultivator, to tear up weeds between crops, improvements in drainage and irrigation works, the introduction of various new types of crops, as well as changes in crop practices etc. We may also add here the development of three-field agriculture in the middle ages which reduced the idleness of arable land by 50 per cent; but any given field was still left uncultivated every third season.[22] This defect was corrected through the introduction of the enclosure in the eighteenth century.

What turned this evolutionary change in agriculture into a revolutionary one was the fundamental change in agrarian organisation and production relations that made possible a sustained growth, a basic condition for the development of modern industries which in turn depended for their sustained expansion on this changed agriculture.

Thus the long process of progress in agriculture through changes in agricultural practices culminated in agricultural revolution when institutional changes were introduced to meet the pressure of population on existing resources. This required the release of resources to be utilised for increasing productivity through technological changes. This whole process, helped by institutional changes, led to the industrial revolution in the eighteenth century.

As such, the most important barrier to the culmination of technical progress since the sixteenth century was small plot size, a condition almost universal in peasant agriculture in the early modern era. There was also no historical need to make the plot larger because of the small population and the nature of the technology of the time. With the increasing pressure of population the disadvantages of this landholding pattern became obvious. The population growth rate in 1740 was not very high, varying between 0.1 and 0.4 per cent per annum. But if we consider the increase in total population resulting from this growth rate in the context of the small size of plot and the low level of technology of the time, we are drawn to the conclusion that this pressure of population meant that institutional changes were needed to make rapid progress in technology effective. Individual farmers on small plots could never introduce sufficiently large amounts of capital equipment into farming practice to lift agricultural production to any major degree. In such circumstances, when total population was growing and consequently more output was desired to feed them, this could only be achieved by utilising more land or trying to elicit modest increases in yield per acre by adding more seed or more labour. 'This condition is equivalent to manufacturing on a handicraft scale—there is no opportunity to introduce steam engines or other major capital goods into the productive process until the jump to large scale factories is made.'[23]

In agriculture, as in industry, this upturn first came in England. Small peasant holdings and common field remnants of feudal agriculture were absorbed and consolidated by large landholders and were literally 'enclosed' with fences. This was first done by voluntary pacts with smaller landholders but in the eighteenth century it was done by an act of Parliament on a petition for enclosure which is more commonly known as parliamentary enclosure. From 1700 to 1845, 14 million acres (i.e. one quarter) of all the arable land were brought together. That the enclosures led to a dramatic increase in productivity is evident from the following calculation: the annual rate of return on investments in enclosure ran as high as 25 per cent, this at a time when the interest rate on government debt instruments was well under 5 per cent.[24] The high yields became the major source of capital improvement and eighteenth-century funds for the construction of canals, roads and irrigation projects. English agricultural entrepreneurs recognised that to use the new machinery they had to have large fields to cultivate because horse-drawn implements could not be manoeuvred in small strips and because only large-scale production could pay off the costs of expensive equipment. In England this organisational change in the form of enclosure was as important as the development of the factory system in industry for creating the institutional pre-conditions for industrialisation and development.

In England, the land was divided into small strips and the holdings of each peasant were scattered in many parts under the feudal domain. There were common pastures and woodlands and there were lands of the lords. From 1700 to 1845, however, land was brought together into large holdings. During this period 14,000,000 acres were enclosed—a quarter of the arable land of the country. In 1873, it is believed, 2,250 persons owned about half the land of England. When tithes were abolished by the Act of 1836 in return for payments, a tendency to increase large holdings was stimulated.

Effects of enclosure on the supply of labour to agriculture have been pointed out by S.B. Clough and C.W. Cole. They stated that for agriculture, as well as for industry, it was important to have a proletariat that was dependent upon a daily wage for a living. In England, this prerequisite of capitalist society was provided by the enclosure acts, which deprived the peasants of the part of the land that they had formerly used, and made them dependent on wages to keep body and soul together. In other places, i.e. France and Germany, where the manorial system disappeared, peasants were not given enough land for their own support or had to pay such large indemnities for living free from rendering services and paying dues to their lords that they soon became landless peasants.[25] This fact accentuated monetisation among rural people and subsequently acted as an incentive to introduce machines when wages began to rise. Initially, however, these landless labourers were engaged in agricultural activities which needed at that time more labour. (For detailed discussions on this aspect see the following sections.)

Organisational change in agriculture played the same role as a precondition for the industrial revolutions in Soviet Russia and China in the twentieth century.

Another important change was the introduction of crop rotation in order to eliminate the idleness of arable land during fallow periods, and this removed a great obstacle to increased productivity in the period. Charles Viscount Townsend (1674-1738) developed rotation into a system and popularised its use, and this is considered as an important factor in the agricultural revolution of the eighteenth century.[26] Rotation helped eliminate the wastefulness of large estates by maintaining the fertility of the soil even if it was made to produce a crop every year. The elimination of the fallow system contributed to the increased demand for labour which had a significant role in the development process.

The combined advantages of a larger scale and the elimination of fallow needed further support from the mechanical aspects of agrarian technology to be effective. Thus the organisational change facilitated the introduction of improved technology.[27] A number of farm implements were invented in England to make farm labour more productive. One of the most important of such inventions was the Norfolk plough which was much lighter than the old and awkward swing ploughs. This is also the period marked by the change from the sickle to the more effective scythe. A further big advance was the development of an entirely iron moldboard and of an all-iron plough (both in 1771). Then came seed drills, horse-drawn hoes, cultivators etc. All these developments led in subsequent periods to the development of a modern iron and steel industry in England, as Bairoch's study has very ably described.[28]

(III) Land Tenure in Eighteenth and Nineteenth Century Europe

Reforms of land tenure and of agricultural organisation have played a vital role in economic development in terms of mobilising resources for more productive utilisation, leading to industrial revolutions. This same role has been played in successful nineteenth-century cases of imported industrialisation, as the French, German, and Japanese cases show.

In the twentieth-century cases of industrial revolution, agrarian reforms again played the most important role in capital formation, although approaches differed from that of the land reform policies of the nineteenth century. The basic role, however, remains the same, as will be evident from the following brief account of land reforms in Europe in the nineteenth century, which might be compared with land reform policies pursued in the Soviet Union and China.

Land reform received serious attention in Europe towards the end of the eighteenth century and at intervals throughout the nineteenth. The policies adopted followed two main patterns. Firstly, steps were taken to turn tenants into owners, thus relieving the cultivators of the burden of the payments in kind or money previously made to landlords. This had the objective of creating an incentive to improve production by the cultivators themselves, as well as enabling them to utilise the surplus that took the form of rent paid to landlords (who used it for conspicuous consumption), for capital formation. Secondly, measures were undertaken to augment the size of peasant holdings by adding to them land taken from large proprietors. This was essential so that mechanisation of agriculture could be made possible so as to release labour and other resources at an increasing rate for the industrial sectors. An illustration is to be found in the expropriation from feudal land owners in France between 1789 and 1793. The land settlements, *Innere Kolonisation*, or small-holdings policies, pursued in Germany, France, Denmark and (though on an insignificant scale) in England, had as their purpose the increase in size of small farms with land compulsorily acquired from large estates. In France and Germany plot size was small compared to England.[29]

Enclosure

The Industrial Revolution required very fundamental changes in land ownership. The very size of the effort of British agriculture implied changes in the size of farms, crop practices, technical and commercial methods etc. 'The fundamental structure of landownership and farming was established by the mid-eighteenth century and certainly by the early decades of the Industrial Revolution. By 1790 landlords owned perhaps three quarters of the cultivated land, occupying free holders perhaps 15 to 20 per cent, and a peasantry in the usual sense of the term no longer existed.'[30]

Enclosure enabled uncultivated land to be brought into use. The charge against enclosure was that it threw peasants off the land when enclosure transformed tilled fields into pastures, but although this happened sometimes, the booming demand for corn meant it was by no means general. Enclosure for tillage, or the use of new rough uncultivated land, actually meant more work rather than less.

The following brief account of enclosure in England as a movement towards large-scale organisation will help in understanding the role of agrarian change, leading to better use of existing resources, as a pre-condition for generating an economic surplus. As mentioned earlier, organisational change created a demand for labour which was of vital importance in terms of subsequent development. Professor Gould has written: 'British agricultural output, until the mid-nineteenth century seems to have risen chiefly by organisational changes (enclosures and tenant farming) and by increasing intensity of cultivation as absolute numbers in agriculture rose,'[31] In underdeveloped countries today, land reform policy (in terms of redistribution of land to actual cultivators, and limiting the size of plot) has failed to create any demand for labour; rather, it has created the problems of increasingly overcrowded small-holdings. In this sense, this policy based on eighteenth and nineteenth-century approaches to agriculture in Europe is proving to have a negative effect. The reason is that industrialisation based on imported resources and technology in these economies has created a very limited demand for labour. In the cases of nineteenth-century imported industrialisation (e.g. France) plot size was initially small after the land reforms, but the growth of industries based on relatively simple and labour-intensive technology, and supported by expanding markets, gradually absorbed surplus labour and evolved as an integrated process of development. The differences in occupational distribution patterns over time in different countries (see Table 2.3) support this contention.

The most dramatic aspect of change in the agrarian framework in England was parliamentary enclosure, the chronology of which was as follows:[32]

Numbers of Enclosure Bills, 1730-1819		Acres of Common Pasture and Waste enclosed by Acts of Parliament	
1730-1759	212	1727-1760	74,518
1760-1789	1,291	1761-1792	478,259
1790-1819	2,169	1792-1815	1,023,634

Parliamentary enclosure would appear as the culmination of a process of land re-allotment, reclamation and fencing into separate parcels, stretching far back in time.[33] It was gradually followed by improvements in tenure and managerial organisation. The latest summary of work on the distinctively English landlord/tenant symbiosis refers to the definite but gradual growth of great estates.[34]

The period between the seventeenth century and 1790 witnessed the growth of the great estates. The estates of the small landowners were also expanding and a class of absentee among them was emerging, but again only gradually.

Tenants did the actual farming, while landowners provided the capital. They brought farm units together in order to make holdings more efficient. Large fixed expenditure on farms was undertaken by the landowners. In this way, the growth of an estate system making it possible for the owner to secure large extra-agricultural revenues for further investment in land proved crucial in raising English agriculture from the rut of capital starvation in which the continental peasantry remained stuck.[35] On the Continent, land reforms did not create large farms. Larger and better-equipped holdings, which were of great benefit to agriculture in England, were the result of the amalgamation of farms and their consolidation from intermixed openfield strips and scattered fields.

G.E. Mingey concludes in his study: 'In general eighteenth century conditions encouraged a persistent bias towards larger farms occupied by tenants rather than free holders.'[36] He further adds, 'there was a long-term tendency towards larger and more efficient units even in openfield villages, and enclosures merely tended to hasten this process'.[37]

The larger farming units were built up by buying out small freeholders and the holdings were then brought together by private exchanges and by enclosure. As the larger farms were more progressive, technically the drift was advantageous.[38]

Had agriculture failed in generating surpluses and feeding the growing population (as it had in the past), industrial development could not have occurred because the population would have been constant with no increase in the labour force, no increased productivity, and no market to provide an incentive. Jones wrote about this period: 'Had agriculture failed in its primary task, so that the population was regularly thinned by famine or alternatively growing equally fast as the supply of food, we need proceed no further. Society would have been so occupied in struggling to maintain output from the land that at most there would have been a minute surplus of income for spending on industrial goods. Economic growth would have been checked by the inflexibility of agri-cultural supply.' This was the fate of France through much of this period (i.e. 1650-1815), just as it is the misery of mankind in many less-developed countries today. English agriculture was more vigorous. It shook off the crisis of subsistence 'which periodically afflicted wide areas of France'.[39]

According to some economists, enclosure in England led to the release of rural labour for factories. This could not happen at the beginning of the enclosure movement because large-scale agriculture with its prevailing level of technology was very labour-intensive.[40] However, G.D.H. Cole wrote that the eighteenth-century enclosures were an important source of a professional class of industrial workers. He wrote: 'The displaced villagers and their children provided the chief supply of labour for the new factories and without their reservoir of disemployed labour the evolution in industry would perforce have been greatly slowed down.'[41] But enclosure movements made large-scale production possible only with the help of labour, albeit more efficiently and productively used. At that time labour-saving machines were not plentiful. But in the course of time, with the progress of industrialisation, there was the necessity to meet the shortage of labour which was the result of rural depopulation. And thus the widespread use of machines began, in the latter part of the nineteenth century in England, and in the 1880s in France and Germany.[42] At the initial stage of the Industrial Revolution in England, 'the first and most obvious shift in the process of production was to utilise more fully the local labour pool. In the labour flush years of the post-Napoleonic war decades farmers were usually able to buy the services of local tradesmen, workers in domestic industry and the wives and children of employees at relatively low cost'.[43]

T.S. Ashton commented on Cole's observation: 'It is true that the larger farms tended to become bigger, but the number small enough to be worked by a single family also increased . . . increasingly as time went on it was the waste that was the subject of the enclosure and the bringing into cultivation of land that had previously hardly been worked at all must have increased employment.'[44]

According to Professor A. Redford, agricultural change at that time more often had the impact of stimulating the growth of the rural population than the reverse, and thus simultaneously with the growth of urban communities, there was also a growth of entirely new agricultural communities as well as the re-enforcement of those already existing.[45]

This might have created a stimulus to early marriage and fertility, leading to growth in the population in urban areas as well as in rural areas. Chambers supported the above view, saying that at some unspecified time in the eighteenth century there was an upward turn in the population in villages beside which the dislocation caused by enclosures was of a secondary importance. Moreover, the evidence of the prevalence of relatively high wages on farms near the industrial centres also indicates that there was a great demand for labour in the villages, and this probably had the effect of stimulating the birth rate in rural areas.[46] Professor Tawney wrote of this time that the problem of population was the problem of underpopulation and contemporary writers were beginning to explore the possibilities of rewards for parents of large families and penalties for bachelors.[47] In the section on China, we have noticed the same trend at the beginning of the industrial revolution there.

Professor E.C.K. Gonner, in his exhaustive studies of census returns, could find no general connection between enclosure and the movement of population away from the land. The expanding and high level of employment maintained both in enclosed and open farming where the improved diversified agriculture was adopted could largely explain the stability of the agrarian population during this period. The explanation seems to be that new agricultural practices had developed in advance of the technical devices for dealing with them.[48]

The widespread use of drilling machinery was a feature of the nineteenth, not the eighteenth century. Thus the yield of corn per acre increased after enclosure but the methods of ploughing, sowing, reaping and threshing were not substantially speeded up until the 1830s and 1840s. Naomie Riches observed that 'when one considers that all the work of ploughing, sowing and harvesting was done with little agricultural machinery, the complexity of labour organisation of these farms becomes intriguing. Imagine harvesting 800 acres of barley by hand i.e. by scythe and sickle and hand made straw bands'.[49]

Enclosures leading to larger-scale operations and diversification of production needed more labour and this increase in demand for labour stimulated the growth of population. The enclosures of Sherwood Forest, Charwood, Enfield Chase, Bere Forest, Beely Heath, and Hampton Common and of wastes in Cumberland, Dorset, Derbyshire, Lancashire, Yorkshire, and Northumberland continued to stimulate the growth of population in rural areas almost up to the middle of the nineteenth century.

Arthur Young (1740-1820), the famous advocate of the new agriculture in England, wrote of that contemporary period, 'in so far as enclosure was associated with capital investment in improved agriculture it was followed not by a decline but by a growth of population'.[50] In his *Northern Tour*, written in 1770, he elaborates on this theme, with a wealth of illustrations, to show that an expanding economy will call into being its own labour supply by providing incentives to early marriage. He writes:

It is employment that creates population: marriages are early and numerous in proportion to the amount of employment. In a great Kingdom, there must always be hands that are idle, backward in the urge to work, unmarried for fear of having families or industrious only to a certain degree. Now an increase of employment raises wages and high wages change the case of all of these hands; the idle are converted to industry; the young came early to work; the unmarried are no longer fearful of families and the formerly industrious become so in a much greater degree. It is an absolute impossibility that in such circumstances the people should not increase . . . Provide new employment and new hands will inevitably follow.

Adam Smith in his *Wealth of Nations* argued in much the same strain that the real rewards of labour had risen, enabling the labourers to provide better for their children, and consequently to bring up a greater number of them.[51] Eden and Malthus related population growth to the greatly increased demand for labour combined with a greatly increased productive ability within agriculture and manufacturing.[52]

It may be concluded that English agriculture successfully played its role in an economy which was growing in all aspects—in population, average income per head and capital stock. This success not only led to the growth of population through increased marriage rates, earlier marriage, falling death rates and increased fertility; it also resulted in supplies of food and raw materials which helped to reduce the upward movement of industrial wages and raw material prices. This in turn led to the increasing consumer demand for industrial goods and thus stimulated industrial expansion. This expansion, being based on simple technology and on the process of using human resources more productively, created an increased demand for labour. Agricultural changes at the time did not release sufficient labour for the urban industries; the enclosure movement was not the institutional means of creating the urban proletariat. Agricultural changes leading to large-scale and diversified farming (e.g. the spread of the turnip cultivation, green fodder crops etc.) needed rural labour, the methods being simple and labour-intensive. This high demand for labour for economic development gradually resulted in increasingly capital-intensive methods of production.

J.D. Chambers points out that modern systems of husbandry (especially the labour-absorbing root crops), reclamation of barren land, and the physical processes of enclosure and improvement (hedging, fencing, building farms and laying out service roads) all demanded more labour, not least where forests, fens and moors were enclosed and reclaimed; according to him, apart from the threshing machine, labour-saving machinery on the farm was not important before the middle of the nineteenth century.[53] Jones referred to Deane and Cole in support of the view that far from the land losing manpower between the first census in 1801 and that of 1815 the absolute numbers engaged in agriculture, forestry and fishing never ceased to climb. They were 1.7 million in 1801 rising to 2.1 million in 1851. However, productivity per capita was also rising alongside total productivity.[54]

The stimulation of rural trades and industries resulting from the increased productivity of farming, the rise in population and the increasing traffic on the roads has also been advanced as one of the causes of the numerical increase of cottage owners. The cottage-owning population showed a continuous growth in enclosed villages.

Nevertheless, although enclosure did not throw labour out of agriculture into the urban works, it did help turn rural workers into wage labourers. The labourer who merely rented property to which common rights once attached and the small tenant farmer whose holding might be amalgamated with others to form bigger units were often converted into workers to be hired and fired at will, a landless rural proletariat. Professor Jones wrote, 'enclosure was not the creator of a labour force for industry. Enclosure itself tended to mop up labour from the countryside'.[55] This is very plausible, as the level of technology prevailing at the early stage of the industrial revolution was low and the economy was rapidly expanding unlike the economies of countries with imported industrialisation. Jones mentioned another but important factor in this respect, i.e. the resistance on the part of general labour to being sucked into the industrial sector. He quoted the following comments of a nineteenth-century Wiltshire incumbent who saw both sides of the enclosure — 'indoor and out-door habits, the loom and the plough, the shuttle and the sickle, the soft hand and the hard hand, cannot be interchanged at pleasure'.[56]

Manufacturers could not draw enough on reserves of rural labour. Arthur Young mentioned in *Of Manufacturers Mixed with Agriculture* the competition for labour between agriculture and industry.[57] It was recorded that throughout the eighteenth century iron furnaces and forges were brought to a seasonal standstill by the preference of their operatives to go harvesting. This is applicable to most manufacturing activities. This demand for labour had a positive impact on the fertility of the population and marriage rates, in both urban and rural areas.

Kuznets' suggested definition of 'the pre-industrial phase' is as follows: the pre-industrialisation phase may be defined as the decade when the share of the labour force in agriculture was at least six-tenths of the total and was just ready to begin its downward movement.[58] The criterion of the rate of change of the proportion of labour in agriculture as well as its level would help us in assessing the effects of an industrial revolution as in England and an imported industrialisation as in France, Germany or Japan. However, the experience of economic development in the nineteenth century tends to suggest that there may be a fairly long gap between the beginning of the process of industrialisation and the point where the sectoral distribution of labour changes sharply. This was due to the fact that the early factories were simple and labour-absorbing. Yet we find a basic distinction in this respect between the case of the classical Industrial Revolution and the cases of imported industrialisation. In England in 1688, at about the beginning of the agricultural revolution, 75 per cent of the working population was engaged in agriculture, and France in 1700 had 80 to 85 per cent of the working population employed in agriculture. Table 2.3 shows the changes in this proportion for England and Wales, France, Germany and Japan and reveals the pattern of industrial development.

Table 2.3: Agricultural Employment as Proportion of Total Employment

Country	Year	Proportion
England and Wales	1841	24
	1861	19
	1881	12
	1901	9
	1950	5
	1962	4
France	1788	75
	1845	62
	1866	52
	1886	48
	1906	43
	1926	39
	1951	27
	1962	20
Germany	1882	42
(Germany was introduced to	1895	36
modern industries in and around	1907	34
the late 1840s and according to		
Rostow the take-off occurred in	1925	30
1850)	1939	27

Country	Year	Proportion
Germany	1950	25
	1962	13
Japan	1877-82	83
	1887-92	76
	1897-1902	70
	1907-12	63
	1920	54
	1940	42
	1953	42
	1962	30

Sources: Simon Kuznets, 'Industrial Distribution of National Product and Labour Force', *Economic Development and Cultural Change* (July 1957), pp. 84, 88, 89 and 91, and *Manpower Statistics, 1950-62* (OECD, 1963).

In earlier cases of imported industrialisation, the rate of change in occupational distribution was slow but steady, with the proportion of agricultural workers declining gradually. When we examine later cases of imported industrialisation in the mid-twentieth century we notice a complete standstill in this respect. If we take account of occupational distribution in these countries on the eve of the introduction of modern industries from the West, we will see that a much larger proportion was engaged in non-agricultural pursuits than today. (See the discussion on India in Chapter 3.)

In sum, commercial farming in England should be considered as an innovation just as surely as the steam engine or the canal. The bulk of enclosure coincided with the classic Industrial Revolution breaking the system of centuries of the feudal tenures in England and was greatly speeded up as demand for food grew first with population and then with industry. The enclosing of common and waste land was done both to create new arable land by improved methods of clearing and draining and to facilitate husbandry of sheep and livestock.

It is, however, to be noted that the greatest movement of enclosures was coincident with the period of the rise of British industry. It meant the final rationalisation of land tenures under the pressure of rising demand with steady growth in population; at the same time it represented a technological revolution and social upheaval as well as indicating the beginning of the Industrial Revolution. The technological side was mainly associated with new methods of husbandry, the right crops for the right soil, rotation of grasses etc.[59]

Improvements in farming techniques and practices, like dill seeding (Tull), root crops (Townsend), late-eighteenth-century drainage techniques (Elkington), new grasses and fodders (Thomas Coke of Holkham), and in the breeding of cattle, horses, and sheep (Blackwell), acted as a stimulus to the English farmers to encourage the reorganisation of agricultural tenures associated with the enclosures. In this way English farms were consolidated and agricultural output increased.

England fed herself in most years until the third decade of the nineteenth century when the responsibility of supplying food to the UK was passed on to the newly settled countries as a part of the practice of the international division of labour as the basis of the international trade. However, at that time, 'the new towns and factories grew without a balance of payments drain for food'.[60] The destruction of feudal land-tenures created a rural proletariat. As farms were consolidated, the yeomanry disappeared. Elimination of the smaller farms meant more efficient farming which at that stage of technology needed more labour in farming the consolidated large farms. Thus more efficient farming supported increasing numbers in the cities and in the countryside as well. The rural proletariat was welcomed as cheap labour but not as a self-sufficient labour force.

The Case of France

In medieval times there was a great similarity of land tenure and of agricultural methods in England and France. In France too, peasant holdings were small and scattered under the feudal domain. But in France, in contrast, movement away from medieval agriculture was much less rapid than in England. Enclosures were relatively few and peasants had not been freed from seignorial obligations to the extent that they had been in England.

The French Revolution, however, did not greatly increase peasant holdings. The results of the French Revolution regarding the landholding as pointed out by Clough and Cole were, (i) that the peasants got title to scattered strips, (ii) that their holdings were increased somewhat, (iii) that the nobles were deprived of some but not all of their estates and (iv) that the Church lost all its land. There were still some large farms, especially around Paris, in the northern plain toward Flanders, and in the west and south west, which were in the hands of the bourgeoisie. The peasants continued to live in villages and to go out to their fields for work. Their holdings were still scattered. The French Revolution led to an important development, i.e. the establishment of a large class of small landowners. In 1882, out of a total of 5,672,007 farms, 4,852,963 were holdings of ten hectares or less.[61]

In France, the change from medieval agriculture was slower than it had been in England. The French landlords were more interested in extracting money payments, services and goods from peasants than in raising productivity, and hence were not in general interested in introducing organisational changes like enclosures.[62]

Overcrowded agriculture coupled with severe oppression by the landlords, however, led to the changes in the agrarian structure and the abolition of feudalism with the French Revolution of 1789. Modern industrialisation did not evolve in France to meet the needs of agriculture but was rather the result of the demonstration effect of the industrial revolution in England.

It has been pointed out by S.B. Clough and R.T. Rapp among others that in France, unlike England, pressure for the acquisition of land to cultivate came from the peasants rather than from landlords. A high density of population, limited opportunities for alternative employment and inequality in its distribution led to a tremendous pressure for arable land. The inequality in distribution can be assessed from the fact that peasants constituted 90 per cent of the population at that time, while they had the right to work only 30 per cent of the land. However, they worked most of the land held by noblemen (which constituted 27 per cent of the total), clerical lands (15 per cent) and the land held by the bourgeois (27 per cent), but their wages were very meagre.[63]

On the eve of the French Revolution, therefore, the peasants' demand was for the abolition of the oppression they had been subjected to, plus the right to more land and with a clear title to it. With the success of the revolution the peasants were granted clear title to their lands without the payment of compensation. As a result a large proportion of the agricultural land of France consisted of small holdings which were obviously not suitable to the introduction of modern methods, such as horse-drawn implements.

According to a census of land holdings, France had more small holdings than most countries, as Table 2.4 shows.

Despite France's great wealth in the early modern period she did not experience the sustained burst of technical change and expansion of output at the time of her industrialisation that had occurred in England. The lack of modernisation of agrarian organisation (i.e. the continuation of small plot size,) was the basic reason for stagnation in agriculture which in turn explains the absence of any demographic revolution of the type that took place in England over the comparable period. In the mid-1850s, when modern industrialisation was under way in France,

Table 2.4:   Landholdings in France

Size of Holdings in hectares (1 hectare = 2.47 acres)	Number of Holdings			
	1862	1882	1892	1908
Very small: less than one		2,167,667	2,235,405	2,087,551
Small: 1—10	2,435,401	2,635,030	2,617,518	2,523,713
Medium: 10—40		636,309	727,222	711,118
Large: 40—100	154,167	142,088	105,391	118,497
Very large: over 100			33,280	
Total		2,672,007	5,702,752	550,544

Source: S.B. Clough and R.T. Rapp, 'Changes in European Land Holdings', *European Economic History* (McGraw Hill, 1975), p. 278.

mostly based on imported resources (i.e. capital, technology, and skill) the rate of natural increase of the population in France was three per thousand whereas in the corresponding years the rate of increase of the population in England and Wales was eleven per thousand. This absence of the 'critical spiral' of early economic growth is the principal cause of the stagnation of the French economy in the nineteenth century; although new industries were developing with the help of imported resources, these were not capable of generating a dynamic growth force as was the case with the English industrial revolution. Population growth in England was a major challenge to the food-producing sector of the economy, comprising nearly 70 per cent of the total population, and resulted in the agricultural revolution leading to the industrial revolution. In France, the pressure of population on resources was not so acute at that time, and in the subsequent period the importation of industrialisation from England negated any possibility of an industrial revolution in France. A dual economy resulted, comprised of a modern but limited industrial sector and a large but small-scale agricultural sector. Thus dualism, however, gave way to the need for integration in a short time because of the increasing absorption of labour from the rural sector by the industrial sector, as the industrial sector of the period was mostly based on simple labour-intensive technology, unlike the post-1950s imported industrialisation in underdeveloped countries.

In England, where the industrial transformation was most rapid, urban centres grew faster than elsewhere in Europe, where industrialisation was a longer and more imitative process. Consequently, in the rest of Europe, the dislocation of the rural-urban shift was less severe and the growth of urban population was relatively slow as is evident from the Table below.

Table 2.5:   Urban Population in Selected Countries as a Percentage of Total Population in 1880

Country	Percentage of Urban Population
England and Wales	67.9
France	34.8
Belgium	43.0
Germany	29.1
Russia	15.0
Denmark	28.0

Sources: UN, *The Determinants and Consequences of Population Trends*, Population Studies no. 17 (NY, UN, 1953), p. 109.

The percentages of urban population in the USA and Canada, where modern industries and agriculture were imported lock, stock and barrel (i.e. skill, labour, technology and capital), were only 28.6 and 15.9 respectively, being mostly composed of immigrants from Europe. The outcome of such transfers was that the possibilities for indigenous growth in these countries were severely limited. Referring to France, Professor Hohenberg wrote that in the nineteenth century 'we are left with a long period of slow change, seemingly little affected by the profound transformation in industry, towns, transportation and trade, let alone by political developments. A possible explanation is that these outside events just did not impinge on the rural economy'.[64]

Hohenberg, however, points out that the above conclusion seems too simple when one takes into consideration the ease of movement of goods and people and even of capital and the high degree of political integration of the country. He therefore concluded that 'rural France cannot have been untouched by the growth of industry, the building of a railroad network, and the shift from protection to free trade and back again'.[65] He argued that the failure of the above events to speed up the pace or to alter the basic direction of change in rural France was due to the fact that their effects operated to confirm the structures and tendencies already present.[66]

This supports the contention of this book that the process of industrial development in France was basically different from that in England in the sense that in the former case it did not emerge to meet the requirements of the rural sector and thus failed to produce that dynamic effect seen in the industrial revolution in England.

It may be argued that in France the population growth was not as pressing as it was in England. Due to the underdeveloped methods of rural production which created uncertainty about the supply of food, there was a tendency among the people to practice population control. Henry Louis wrote, 'birth control began to spread among the mainly rural mass of the population. This period marked the beginning of the decline in the French birth rate which occurred so much earlier than in other European countries'.[67] This was achieved mainly by the relative lateness of marriage. It has been pointed out that celibacy, both ecclesiastical and secular, has been described as the malady characteristic of the period and a great danger to the growth of the French population.

The above phenomenon might be explained with the help of two factors; on the one hand the small plot size of French farming which could not support an increasing population without increasing misery, and on the other, the growth of industries with a relatively limited demand for labour, the result of transplantation. Overcrowded agriculture failed to create the conditions for an industrial revolution as industrialisation had already been transplanted into the urban sectors to satisfy the interests of merchants, bourgeois and landlords. This attracted people to urban areas for employment, the scope of which was, however, limited, but much larger than in today's so-called urban centres in underdeveloped countries due to the differences in the capital intensity of technology in the two periods. Hohenberg wrote about France: 'The urban population rose from some 7 million in 1821 to 17.5 million in 1911 and the rise in urban incomes doubled the increase in the markets for food due to numbers of people. Towns became more urban, more detached from local and informal sources of agricultural produce, and thus more dependent on full time farmers.'[68] Hohenberg also mentioned that more people left rural France between 1851 and 1856 than in any other intercensal period before 1914.[69] (Almost 400,000 people were lost through 'net migration' with an 1851 population of 22.4 million.)

France experienced the beginnings of modern industrialisation on a large scale around 1850, nearly eighty years after England. Whereas the dual change (i.e. agricultural revolution and industrial revolution) in England seems to have been strongly stimulating to economic growth and development, the results in France are far less clear cut due to the different pattern of change, as maintained earlier, which had a limited effect on employment. The generally negative effect of industrialisation, based on imported capital, on rural economic activity might be considered as the basic reason behind the differences in the two outcomes. Cottage industry gave way to factories, rural artisans found their local market invaded by factory-produced goods and industries based on limited resources, such as iron works, were quickly overrun.[70]

Modern transport, railroads in particular, displaced a sizeable labour and animal-using carrying trade that had flourished on the roads and inland waterways.[71] As this modern transport was based on imported capital and skill, its growth created relatively limited alternative employment opportunities for these displaced workers, unlike in England. A number of tertiary occupations lost ground due to the greater accessibility of urban services as a result of modern transport and communication, and also due to stagnating agriculture. Had modern industrialisation in France evolved indigenously, the employment effects would have probably been different. However, compared to the employment effects of imported industrialisation in the Third World since the 1950s, they were more positive in the 1850s due to the differences in the level of technology of the two periods and due to the fact that imported capital at that time was paid for by exports, unlike the unlimited availability of foreign capital, technology and skill in underdeveloped countries today in the form of foreign aid, foreign investment etc. The industries imported today are highly sophisticated and capital-intensive.

Agriculture in France at that time was based on labour-using rather than labour-saving processes, as was the case with the enclosures, or land reorganisation policy in England. In England, however, enclosure led to large-scale organisation while in France land reform policy led to generally small plot size, but 'the reduction in fallow, higher grain yields, better working of the soil and larger numbers of farm animals attendant on the introduction of new rotations led to increasing labour absorption, even when landscape was not transformed as by enclosure'.[72] This marks another difference with unsuccessful cases of imported industrialisation in the twentieth century.

In France, low fertility, as mentioned earlier, reduced the supply of labour, and on the demand side, the pull was not strong due to the slow change in agriculture. Due to the process of industrialisation in France, the pool of non-agricultural rural labour was large enough. However, in England rapid population growth went at least some way to bring supply into balance with demand, which was much greater due to the simultaneous development of agriculture, industry and commerce in the process of the industrial revolution. The pull of demand for labour was strong in all sectors of the economy.

In France at this time capital left agriculture as peasants saved to buy land from those who left. In other words, rural France provided capital to the urban sector, though the real investment largely took place outside France altogether (i.e. this resource was largely used to buy imported capital, skill and technology, products of real investment elsewhere, which as a consequence could not produce any dynamic force for development). Therefore rural France lost the investment needed from additional savings, which did not materialise due to the pattern of development.[73] In underdeveloped countries today a very small part of the rural people (i.e. rich land owners and traders) save and invest but they do so in urban areas and not in agriculture.[74] The large majority of peasants can hardly eke out a subsistence living from their farming, therefore the question of saving and its investment is immaterial.

Bairoch has argued, as we have noted before, that early industrialisation, particularly iron production, depended heavily on rural demand, but rural France provided little impetus, lacking a market for industrial goods. Outside agriculture, economic life in rural areas, including market towns, was at best stagnant.[75]

What was the condition of farming in England at a comparable stage? At the beginning of industrial development, 'we can hardly any longer speak of a British peasantry' in the same sense that we can speak of a French, German or Russian peasantry: farming was already predominantly for the market, manufacture had long been diffused through a countryside no longer feudal. Agriculture was already prepared to carry out its three fundamental functions in an era of industrialisation: to increase production and productivity, so as to feed a rapidly rising non-agricultural population; to provide a large and rising surplus of potential recruits for the towns and industries; and to provide a mechanism for the accumulation of capital to be used in the more modern sectors of the economy.[76]

The Case of Germany

In the early nineteenth century, Germany was an agricultural country. Approximately 75 per cent of the population lived in rural areas. Most of the agricultural land was the property of the aristocracy except in the Rhineland provinces and south-western Germany where much of the land was owned by the small farmers. The feudal order on the land was the cornerstone of Prussian society in the eighteenth century. In France, the feudal system had been destroyed in the revolutionary edicts of August 1789, August 1792 and July 1793 and confirmed in the *code Napoléon* in 1804. In Prussia, the system remained virtually intact. Peasants lived in a condition of hereditary serfdom, the forms of the serfdom varying in different areas. They were unable to move or marry, without the permission of the lords to whose estates or person they were bound. Their children were obliged to work on these estates. Even those peasants who owned land were forced to provide labour service on the aristocratic (*Junker*) estates and their ownership of land depended on the performance of their future duties.[77]

After the crushing defeat of Prussia by the French in 1806 and the crop failure of 1816 important measures for economic growth and modernisation of Germany were introduced. The most important of these was the Prussian edict of 14 September 1814 which revised the relationship between landlord and peasant and which called for the liberation of serfs.

The liberation of serfs was an important step towards the economic and social development of Prussia. The major contribution in this respect was in the form of the mobility of occupation and labour force, one of the most important conditions for the modern industrial development of a country. The feudal mode of production now belonged to the past. But the subsequent reform did not help servile peasantry to emerge as a class of fiercely independent yeomen farmers. The free peasant was too weak to compete with large landowners in a free market economy. Small farmers' holdings after the edicts of 1811 and 1816 were too small to support a family adequately and thus they had no capital. Credit was available at a high rate of interest from money lenders who thus proved to be the cause of the family's downfall. Kitchen wrote: 'By contrast the aristocracy had their own credit institutions which provided them with much of the capital required for expansion and for investment in modern techniques.'[78] The effects of land reforms thus made for the diminution of the amount of the land owned by the peasantry and the enlargement of the size of the holdings of the Junkers. The Junkers speculated in the land on the free market and bought up the holdings of the peasants who were forced to sell due to the acute economic difficulties and agricultural crises of the 1820s. According to accounts of most historians about 45 per cent of all peasant land (amounting to about 2.5 million acres) was thus lost to the Junkers. Thus the large estates of the Junkers, the product of feudalism, grew larger as a result of the land reforms introduced during the early nineteenth century, unlike France where estates were divided up among the peasantry. However, in Prussia, the large feudal estates became capitalist concerns.

In England, however, estates were leased out to enterprising farmers who contributed substantially to the Industrial Revolution.

In Prussia, the peasants who became mostly free wage-earners made an important contribution as a source of labour to the subsequent course of industrialisation, inputs of which were mostly imported, and the process of industrialisation of the period was obviously labour-intensive.

It is, however, to be noted here that elements of the old system still remained although land reforms during the early decades of the nineteenth century led to the abolition of serfdom throughout Germany. The freedom of the peasantry was restricted until the revolution of 1848 when the old reluctantly gave way to the new.

Germany's Land Reorganisation. In Germany, as in France, plot size was small after land reform policies were adopted and there was pressure of population on these plots.[79] However, there were large plots of land in Prussia east of the Elbe, but in the west and south-west, along the Rhine, the Main, and the Neckar Rivers, small holdings were more usual.

Table 2.6:   Land Holding in Germany

Area of Tillage, 1807	Hectares (in millions)	Proportion of Holdings, as percentages of Total			
		Up to 12.5	12.5-50	50-250	Over 250 Hectares
East of Elbe	13.9	8.5	22.7	28.5	40.3
West of Elbe	17.9	22.0	40.0	30.0	8.0

Source: S.B. Clough and R.T. Rapp, *European Economic History* (McGraw Hill, 1975), p. 279.

On the banks of the Rhine, small peasant proprietorships were created when the Federation was abolished in 1798. To the east of the Elbe, serfdom was abolished under the edicts (1807-9) of Baron von Stein. In these areas landlords were allowed to create large holdings.

But in Germany, as in France, with increasing industrial activities in urban areas the demand for food expanded; whereas previously the small grain harvest had been the main farm operation, the demand for food created exceptional demand for labour. In Germany between 1816 and 1861 the agricultural labour force increased by 23 per cent and the crop demand by 60 per cent. From 1850 to 1880 this gap widened as rural population growth slowed down and the crop demand increased by 50 per cent.[80] The same trend was visible in contemporary France.

A brief note on industrial transplantations in France and Germany has been included in the following section to explain the nature of imported industrialisation in nineteenth-century Europe and its implications for the cases of imported industrialisation in the twentieth century.

(IV) Industrial Transplantation in France and Germany

France

Henderson has observed that 'during the hundred years between 1750 and 1850 Britain not only became the leading manufacturing country in the world but her inventors, skilled mechanics and entrepreneurs exercised a profound influence upon the industrialisation of the Continent and the United States of America'. Britain was the source of skills and capital to all those countries that followed her in building their railways, iron and steel, textile and machine-making industries.

The development of the French textile industries owed much to British machinery, technical knowledge and textile workers. According to Henderson 'by the middle of the eighteenth century the trickle of skilled English textile workers migrating to France has assumed greater proportions'.[81]

In A.P. Wadworth and J. de L. Mann's *The Cotton Trade and Industrial Lancashire 1600-1780* (1931), there is a detailed account of the transfer of capital, skilled workers and technology from England to France in the development of the cotton, jute and textile industries in the nineteenth century.

In the eighteenth century the iron and steel industry was backward when compared with that of England.[82] But in the late eighteenth and early nineteenth century, English capital and exports played a vital role in the growth of this industry.[83] Michael Alcock, an English metal worker, was one of the leading entrepreneurs in the French metal working, engineering and machine-building industries. French scientists and technicians were also sent to England to study modern methods of iron production.[84] The introduction into France of steam pumps and steam engines to drive machinery was another step on the road to industrialisation. These new machines, however, came from Britain. James Watt's rotative steam engine was introduced into France by Francois Grace de Mendel. Not only machines were imported from England to France during this time; a large number of English workers were also employed in many French industrial establishments. It has been stated in a French journal (*Annales d'Industrie et de l'étranger*) that Manley and Wilson at Charenton in 1842-5 employed 350 British and 350 French workers. There were many English engineers active in Paris in the 1820s and 1830s. Henderson wrote that British capital, technical knowledge and skilled labour were of considerable significance in the early development of French railways. The Minister of Public Works set up a commission in 1833 to study future French railway routes and engineers were sent to England to examine recent railway development there. It was not until August 1837 that the first Paris railway was opened. One of the first engine drivers was an Englishman named John English.

Henderson concluded his studies of the English influence on French industrial development as follows: 'Between 1750 and 1850 the "industrial revolution" in France was fostered by English invention and English capital and by the services of English entrepreneurs, contractors and skilled workers'.[85] As in Germany and Japan, the French government fostered industrial progress.

Wolfnam Fisher wrote that industrialisation on the Continent was not initiated by private enterprise alone as in the British Isles, but was essentially assisted by government activity. According to W.O. Henderson, one of the foremost experts in the comparative economic history of Europe in the nineteenth century, on the Continent the state played a much more active part in fostering economic progress than was customary in England or Scotland in the early nineteenth century.[86] In cases of imported industrialisations, the state must have to play a relatively significant role for reasons stated earlier (p. 11).

Germany

A combination of the new and the old has been, and is, a characteristic of any developing economy. A sharp contrast — of the kind described by economists as dualism — is the sign of incomplete industrialisation and is particularly associated with economies that are in the process of rapid change, for example Japan and Germany. German development was a conscious decision. It was carried out within each state by an autocrat and was systematic and designed to achieve a definite end. In this it has a close similarity with the modern Japanese development process.

David Landes has pointed out that in the beginning several rural areas were already characterised by overpopulation and chronic underemployment and this was the slack to be taken up. There was steadily increasing population beyond the capacity of agriculture to absorb. Importation of industries from Britain and subsequently from other parts of Europe (i.e. France and Belgium) helped in absorbing this surplus labour. The import of skills and other resources enabled Germany successfully to overcome her backwardness. Agriculture was tapped to pay for these imported resources. Improved transport (through imported railways) and a politically unified market (*Zollverein*) provided the stimulus for rapid industrialisation based on imported human and material resources.[87]

Partly because German development was so late, it had a clear purpose and could see where it was going. Compare English education, which had been sheer compromise, with the systematic reconstruction of the educational system by Prussia (from the Universities downwards), with compulsory attendance as long ago as 1808. In Germany the State was all powerful, not indifferent to industrial progress as was the Government in *laissez faire* England. It was eager to aid the progress of industry by all means at its disposal (e.g. tariffs, bounties etc.). In the iron and steel industry Germany had the advantage of starting late and learning from England as it did in the engineering, chemical and textile industries.

W.O. Henderson wrote: 'In Hamburg in 1841 the firm of Gliechmen and Busse worked "with English iron, with English coals, and with English models". All their tools were English, their director was an Englishman and of the 150 hands who were in their employment, 90 were likewise English'.

There are numerous examples of this sort of transfer of technology, capital and skill from England to Germany and other continental countries in the nineteenth century. Henderson made a detailed study of the industrial transplantations to Germany from Britain in the nineteenth century which initiated their modern industrialisation. The following excerpts will help toward the better understanding of the nature of such transplantation.[88]

By the early 1840s half of Germany's iron and iron products came from abroad (55 per cent in 1843). The *Zollverein's* iron imports (in terms of pig iron) rose from 900,000 cwt in 1839 to 4,200,000 cwt in 1843. The British iron industry, then the greatest in the world, contributed the lion's share of Germany's iron imports. The quality of some of the products of the German iron industry were far from satisfactory in the early nineteenth century. The modernisation of Germany's old fashioned iron works—small foundries and forges situated in remote wooded valleys and still smelting with charcoal—was an essential feature of the 'German industrial revolution'.

The German jute industry was also started with English capital but with Scottish experts. Julius Spiegelberg, after visiting Scotland to study the industry, set up the first German jute spinning factory at Vechelde near Brunswick in 1861. Dundee jute spinners trained the German workers. The necessary capital was not forthcoming in Germany but Spiegelberg was able to secure it by the establishment of the British and Continental Jute and Flax Works Co. Ltd in London.

Germany's first machine-building establishment was set up in 1819, with the help of engineers, moulders, mechanics, steam engines and various other machines brought from England. English influence was also evident in other early German machine-making establishments. In Berlin, John Cockerell and Biram set up factories to build textile machinery. There are numerous examples of such transplantations to Germany. German governments worked actively to foster industrial progress by assisting industrialists through subsidies, and licenses to import machinery duty free and also by sending experts abroad to study foreign technology.

British capital, skill and labour played an important part in the development of railways, steam navigation and of public utilities such as gas and water. British influence was great on the commercial and industrial development of Germany.

Imported industrialisation has been fostered everywhere by direct and indirect state participation. Another characteristic of such industrialisation is that production and the market in major industrial activities is dominated by monopolies as a result of economic forces.[89]

The dualistic pattern of German industrial development has been pointed out by other authors. According to Kitchen, German economic development from the 1840s was relatively rapid and very uneven. Industrial productivity grew far more rapidly than agricultural productivity creating something of an imbalance which may be described as dualistic in the sense the term is used today in economic development.

The Prussian way to modernisation, with the great estates of the landowning aristocracy still showing remnants of the feudal order, feudal estates gradually becoming capitalist junker estates, was part of the reason for this slow development. As expected in the case of an imported industrialisation, within industry it was heavy industry — meaning iron and steel and mechanical engineering — which led the way, and not light as in the English Industrial Revolution. The transport industry, particularly the railways consumed the bulk of investment capital and acted as a major stimulus to economic growth.[90]

The implications of such industrial transplantation in Germany in its early stage of industrialisation, as shown very briefly above, are discussed in Chapter 3.

(V) The Pattern of Development in Japan

Introduction

There is numerous evidence to show that Japan had an expanding proto-industrial sector just on the eve of the Meiji Restoration in 1868 indicating that Japan's own pre-industrial technological and commercial growth attained a level almost similar to that of England on the eve of the Industrial Revolution. E.S. Crawcour wrote:

> Industry had become widely diffused throughout most of Japan by the mid-nineteenth century. This diffusion rather than any great technological progress was the main feature of industrial development in traditional Japan. At the beginning of the Tokugawa period in the early seventeenth century, when the mass of the population still lived by subsistence farming and demand for most industrial products was practically confined to aristocrats and feudal courts, industry was mostly of the craft type and existed only in a few centres such as Kyoto and the Castle towns. By the mid-nineteenth century, however, industries once the jealously guarded preserve of groups of craftsmen under empirical or feudal patronage had spread widely through towns and villages over most of the country. This spread was mostly connected with the spread of the commercial economy.[91]

It is evidence of changes in methods of production, but not of a transformation of the industrial structure.[92] The condition closely resembles what Hobsbawm wrote about the British economy on the eve of the Industrial Revolution in his *Industry and Empire.* But the pressure of population, the growth rate of which was even less than 0.5 per cent per annum or less than 10 per cent in two decades from 1852 to 1872, was not enough to stimulate the level of proto-industrial activities to industrial activities through changes in economic organisation and technology.[93] Agrarian structure was also at the pre-industrial feudal stage.

But when the Meiji Restoration took place in 1868 modern technology and capital was accepted in the name of modernisation so that 'a strong and rich nation' could evolve mainly out of fear of domination by foreigners. Thus the industrialisation in Japan had no indigenous root despite the fact that she had a well developed proto-industrial economy.

Japan's policy of importing technology and capital from industrialised countries of the time made her hopelessly dependent on imported raw materials since the period of the Meiji Restoration. Had Japan's industrialisation process evolved from her proto-industrial stage as a result of improvement in technology in agriculture and proto-industries, Japan's dependence on raw materials for her industrialisation process would not have been so severe as it is today.

It has been pointed out by economists that 'Japan is perhaps the

classic example in economic development of a move into industrialisation from an "in between" position. She was not so far along economically as the early industrialisers of Western and Central Europe in their
pre-industrial phases, nor was she so backward as most of the countries
of Asia and Africa today'.[94] This observation is justified when we compare the stage of the economy and technology in the late nineteenth
century with that of the industrialised nations of the time. But when
we compare pre-industrial stages of Japan and the UK we find a close
similarity in level. In my opinion, the missing link was the rate of growth
of population which was not sufficient to spur agriculture and proto-
industries to the industrial technology.

Japan is the only country which has developed a successful industrial
economy without an industrial revolution in this century. However, the
process of her industrialisation, which was initiated in the late nineteenth
century, followed closely the pattern of the nineteenth-century industrial
latecomers, i.e. in being based on imported technology and capital. Modern industrial sectors in these countries have been established and
expanded with the concomitant effects of dualistic development between
the modern and the traditional sectors. In Japan this dichotomous
character was not as prominent as it is today in underdeveloped countries
and this may be explained by the vast difference in the capital intensity
of technology between the two periods. This increasingly capital and
consequently energy-intensive technology has been the result of two
historical factors; first, industrialisation has remained confined to a
handful of countries since the industrial revolution, as a direct result of
the international division of labour, which entailed a high growth rate
in these industrialised countries; and second, the declining population
growth rate resulting from the negative fertility effects of capitalist
production and consumption.[95]

In Japan, the manufacturing sector did not evolve as a means to
meet the growing needs of the agricultural sector, but was simply a case
of transplantation from abroad. Thus industrial development in Japan
is not a product of an industrial revolution despite the fact that the
Meiji Restoration in Japan fulfilled two important tasks of an industrial
revolution, namely: (i) centralisation of political power, and (ii) concentration of economic surplus and savings lying scattered in the
feudal structure of the society to make industrialisation a possibility.
As Japanese history showed these two steps proved successful in
achieving a process of industrialisation. But for the successful completion of an industrial revolution the following conditions must be
met.

First, the agricultural structure and organisation must be made more productive so that more resources can be released for technological development and industrialisation.

Second, the manufacturing or industrial sector must be the product of the needs of the primary sector, the largest sector, and be based essentially on indigenous resources. Borrowed technology and capital will result in dualism and monopolistic economic organisation in a prematurely capitalist economy, thus retarding the best possible utilisation of resources.

Thirdly, the fulfilment of the above criteria requires fundamental social and economic change. This did not happen in Japan.

The following analysis of these aspects in Japanese development will be dealt with in more detail in terms of (i) political and economic change, (ii) agriculture, and (iii) the industrial transplantation, in the historical context.

The Japanese development pattern has been aptly characterised by Otsuka Hisao and is as follows. In Japan, the Meiji Restoration took place in 1868 and was the starting point of modernisation in Japan. But when we compare the Meiji Restoration with 'bourgeois revolutions' in western Europe, we find that the former is of a considerably different historical nature in the sense that in the case of the bourgeois revolutions of western Europe modernisation and industrialisation went hand in hand, promoting each other's progress, while in Japan after the Meiji Restoration, as is well known, a certain characteristic alienation between the processes of modernisation and industrialisation appeared. In Japan, after the Restoration, industrialisation and in particular certain types of machine-industry showed marked development, and although Japan even passed through a 'spurt' period and produced a number of modern enterprises, the agricultural sector and the remainder of the manufacturing sector remained almost entirely unaffected by these developments. Though by means of limited industrialisation a partial breakaway from traditional institutions was effected, the framework of the traditional social system, with its main base in the agricultural village, was preserved intact up to the time of the land reform and the dissolution of monopolies after the Second World War.[96]

The Politico-economic Changes

The Meiji Restoration Government's politico-economic policy may be summed as follows:

(i) It abolished feudalism and established the political unification of the country by replacing old titles to authority with the prefectures, i.e. the centralisation of political power was achieved; it also removed the old feudal restraints and pressures and thus each citizen could freely display his zeal for enterprise; freedom of choice of occupation was granted, all limitations on the use of land were removed; respect for private property became general.

(ii) The samurai class was abolished along with their special privileges and pensions.

These changes had the effect of abolishing feudalism's great economic waste and making more productive use of population of formerly unproductive sectors when a centralised and integrated political authority was established. In June 1870, the clans were replaced by the prefecturial system of government—and so modern central government was established. This resulted in a change from the self-sufficient economic units of almost three hundred clan lords to an economy where the whole country was one economic unit.

The clan lords completely lost their traditional ruling authority over the clan, samurai, general public, the lands. New administrative areas were set up for cities and prefectures. Their administrative heads were appointed to fixed terms as governors by the central government. The system of authority was fully centralised.[97]

The modern Western technology and capital were transplanted from Europe with a view to increasing productivity under the initiative and leadership of the state. This required the concentration of the economic surplus that was scattered and not productively utilised. The economic benefit deriving from the abolition of feudalism was the great progress in the use and accumulation of capital. The reform of the samurai's pensions brought an end to a hereditary privilege which had no productive function at all. The samurai's pensions, now converted into bonds, became effective new capital resources. The land with the restrictions on buying and selling removed became an economic asset that could be used as people thought best. Thus these two resources provided the large supply of capital needed for economic growth, and their rational use was advanced one step further by the development of banks and joint stock companies.[98]

G.C. Allen observed that 'the banking system introduced in the early seventies was modelled on the national banking system of the United States. A few years later the government noted that the technical requirements of that system provided an opportunity for solving, in part, its most urgent social and political problem. It turned "samurai" into bankers by contriving that the bonds issued to them in place of their annual pensions could be used as cover for the note issue. Similarly, samurai were found jobs in the government factories—at the artisan as well as at the managerial level. They were assisted financially and in other ways to start new enterprises on their own.'[99]

Agricultural Development in Japan

Fundamental institutional changes in agriculture are considered indispensable steps towards releasing resources for industrialisation, and thus the economic reorganisation of agriculture is considered as the basic key to the development of indigenous technology.

In the case of Japan, the institutional reforms introduced during this period were not of any fundamental importance in terms of the economic organisation of agriculture. Thus we find tenurial relationships were left unchanged. The tenant farmers continued to pay their rent in kind to their landlords and their position remained extremely insecure.[100] The proportion of the area of land under tenant farmers increased from 37 per cent in 1883-4 to 45 per cent by 1903.[101] Instances of parasitic, indifferent, conservative or absentee landlords were numerous.[102] Under the prevailing system of tenancy, farming expenses including the cost of implements, seeds and fertilisers had to be paid by the tenants. Dore wrote: 'Tenants had to borrow money at high interest from the landlord or the fertiliser merchant and the harvest, when it came, left him little better off than before by the time he had paid not only his rent but his fertiliser debts as well.'[103] In extreme cases, the share of the harvest going to the tenant was barely sufficient to pay for the cost of the manure applied to the fields. Because of the financial hardships, the tenants found it hard to keep up with the progress of the times and such poverty was shared by small freeholders. Indebtedness, the mortgaging of their land, and eventually the transfer of ownership was a recurring pattern.[104]

According to W. McCord, 'The Meiji rulers accumulated their investment capital essentially by squeezing peasantry.'[105] This view is also shared by many other economists Japanese and non-Japanese.

According to Paul Baran, 'it is no exaggeration to say that the main source of primary accumulation of capital in Japan was the village which in the course of its entire modern history played for the Japanese capitalism the role of an internal colony'.[106] In other words, according to these authors, although agriculture played an important part in the process of transplantation of industries from abroad, this was effected not through agricultural development but through severe measures leading to the mobilisation of resources from the agricultural sector.

K. Ohkawa and H. Rosovsky argued that in the early stages the agricultural surplus, through government taxation (primarily the land tax), was channelled into non-primary production.[107] They explained that expansion subsequent to the 1880s was due to a movement away from traditional production and toward the more capital-intensive techniques of the modern industrial sector. In their view, the high level of savings in the economy that made this expansion possible depended on a rapidly growing agricultural surplus.

But the interpretation of J. Nakamura, T. Oshima and R.P. Sinha was quite different.[108] In Nakamura's view there is no doubt that the agricultural sector remained the primary source of investment resources; but this surplus or savings growth depended primarily on getting hold of an increasing share of the existing surplus. This contrasts with Ohkawa and Rosovsky's analysis that the increase in savings or surplus is based on obtaining a share of a rapidly expanding surplus production.

It has been pointed out that in the land tax the Meiji rulers did not find a new source of revenue, they merely rationalised an old one, and the land tax was not even adequate to meet the armament requirements of the regime.[109]

It is true that agriculture did make some positive contributions, but if we take the role of large food imports during this period into consideration it would be a clear overstatement that Japanese agriculture provided sufficient food and adequate capital or foreign exchange for modern economic development.

The traditional view of Japanese agricultural development in the Meiji era, suggesting an annual rate of growth of agricultural output of two per cent or more (Ohkawa and Rosovsky) has been seriously challenged by Nakamura. According to Nakamura, agricultural output could not have grown more than one per cent per annum in the entire period.[110] This destroys the traditionalists' thesis regarding the strategic role of agricultural development in the growth of Japan. Moreover, if we examine the period after 1918-20, when the industrial sector has become more or less self-sufficient in the sense that it exports enough to pay for imports required by the industrial sector of the economy, we notice the increasing poverty of Japanese agriculture. The only explanation is that in the process of industrial development agriculture was exploited to mobilise resources to pay for the imports of industrial inputs, and little effort was made to develop agriculture and generate surplus. We notice from the following tables a downward trend in agricultural output after 1919. Obviously, had agricultural development contributed to the development of the Japanese industrial sector, the trends in agricultural output and the pattern of resource utilisation should have been completely opposite.

Table 2.7:   Total Changes in Terms of Average Annual Rates of Growth
              (Agriculture)

	Farm value of production (in percentage)	Value added
1877-1919	1.78	1.88
1919-1938	0.77	0.46

Table 2.8:   Productivity Index

Period	Output index	Productivity index	Gross value added
1877-1885	2.18	2.03	2.34
1885-1894	1.67	1.50	1.49
1894-1905	1.85	1.43	1.73
1905-1919	2.24	1.48	1.78
1919-1931	0.95	0.50	0.52

Source: Ohkawa *et al.*, *Agricultural Growth and Economic Development in Japan*
(Princeton University and Tokyo University Press, 1970), pp. 6, 7.

It is evident from Tables 2.7 and 2.8 that agricultural output showed
considerable gains during the first phase of industrialisation, which could
be due to the backlog of unutilised innovations introduced during the
pre-Meiji period resulting in increased agricultural output, as their use was
stimulated by the more severe measures for the mobilisation of resources
during the Meiji period.

Political measures taken during the Meiji period played an important
role. Political unification of the country, the removal of restrictions on
the internal movement of agricultural products, the provision of means
of transport and communications, the opening up of the country to
foreign trade and the growing foreign demand for silk must have combined to act as a catalyst. But growth was facilitated mainly by the
presence of unutilised technological innovations in the agricultural
sector. However, these technological changes from the pre-Meiji period
did not initiate any structural change in the economy, as evident from
the sectional distribution of the labour force, with 93 per cent of the
labour force depending on agriculture even in the 1890s. This technological change was very simple, mainly seen in the changes in crop
patterns and improvements in tools, that characterise the pre-industrial
days of an agricultural economy. This points to the fact that the

industrialisation process that was introduced during the Meiji period did not evolve from the technological innovation of the Tokugawa period. In that case, industrialisation in Japan would have an indigenous base and would not have been a product of transplantation. In such cases, the development of agriculture remains blocked. Here Japanese industrialisation differs from the classical as well as the twentieth century cases of industrial revolution. In these cases, agricultural development leads to an industrial revolution. Food imports in Japan's early period of industrialisation played the most crucial role of feeding the growing urban population, proving that agricultural development did not lead to the industrialisation of Japan.

The food import figures during this period (given below) show that however fast the agricultural sector grew, it did not provide sufficient food to feed the growing population in the secondary and tertiary sectors.

Food Imports 1894-1903

(a) Net food imports (a) 24 per cent of total imports
　　　　　　　　　　 (b) 28.6 per cent of total export earnings
(b) Rice imports per head of population – 10.68 lbs.
(c) Sugar imports per head of population – 10.04 lbs.
　　(Rice imports per head of population increased to 17.94 lbs in the period 1902-14).

It is to be noted that India imported 21.54 lbs of food grains per head per annum during the early stage of its economic planning for industrialisation (i.e. between 1951-66).[111]

According to Ohkawa, on average 8.3 million people belonging to the secondary and tertiary sectors had to be provided with food annually. On the basis of this estimate, we can conclude that 700 calories per day per head were provided by imports, which means that at least a third of the food consumption of the gainfully occupied population in these two sectors was met by imports.[112]

From 1894 onwards, the number employed in the secondary and tertiary sectors appears to have increased by about 0.22 million per year, the total increase in the period between 1893 and 1914 having been estimated at 4.41 million. But from the point of view of evaluating food requirements this increase should be regarded as cumulative, as the additional employees of the first year have still to be fed in subsequent years. That means an additional 0.22 million employees had to be fed by 1895, 0.44 million by 1886, 0.66 million by 1897 and so on to 4.41

million by 1914. This sum gives a better idea of the total food requirements. When compared with food imports during this period (summed up in the same way), it reveals that if the imported food had been allocated to the additional employees in these sectors each would have received slightly over 2,600 calories, more than 500 calories in excess of the most optimistic estimates of calorific intake for that period. It can be concluded that after 1893 domestic agriculture failed to provide the additional food required for the growing numbers employed in the secondary and tertiary sectors. The task was left to imports, which were by no means moderate.[113]

Most of the imported food was meant for the growing needs of the urban sector. In terms of economic development, it implies that agriculture did not play the traditional role of supplying resources for industrialisation. In other words, industrialisation in Japan did not evolve to meet the needs of agricultural development, and therefore does not comply with our conditions for a complete industrial revolution.

Industrial Transplantation in Japan

Until around the third decade of the Meiji era most of the newly rising industries were enterprises in which the Japanese had had no previous experience. Success or failure was most uncertain and therefore the sense of risk was strong. But the major task of this transplantation was undertaken by the state itself initially, until a Westernised educated elite evolved, with samurais engaged in commercial and financial ventures, and this task of transplantation was handed over to them by the state.

The entire process reveals a basic pattern of industrialisation that did not evolve out of the needs of the primary sector, which was the largest sector of the economy, absorbing more than 90 per cent of the total population.

As regards the transplantation of Western technology, Japan's economic growth since the Meiji period has been a process of catching up with the more industrialised countries. This process has been referred to as a 'technological borrowing' or simply imitation.[114]

The backlog in Japan may be classified into two periods: (i) early Meiji Restoration period, or the initial period of industrialisation, when Japan faced the gap between its technology and the internationally available technology from the West; (ii) post World War II period, when Japan found itself at a technological disadvantage relative to the advanced countries which benefited from being international markets. (See Table 2.9.)

Table 2.9: Kinds of Industries Transplanted to Japan and Transfer Period

Period	Average Years from Invention in Foreign Countries to Industrial Transplant to Japan		Share of Main Introduced Technologies	Share by Period of Introduced Technologies (% Total Number of Technologies, 312)
	A	B		
Before the Restoration 1550-1867	95.4	130	Optical machine technology (36%) Spinning machine technology (18%) Printing, business machine (18%)	5
Industrialisation period in Japan after the Restoration 1868-1900	64.7	68.8	Traffic means & power (17%) Inorganic chemistry technics (14%) Mining technology (13%) Spinning machine technology (9%)	24
Heavy industrialisation period of Japan 1901-14	39.2	39.8	Organic chemistry technology (21%) Traffic means & power, iron & steel technology, organic chemistry technology, plastics (all 9%)	16
Between World War I and World War II 1915-40	34.9	36.6	Inorganic chemistry technology (14%) Communication technology (13%) Traffic means & power, iron & steel technology, organic chemistry technology, plastics (all 9%)	26
From World War II to postwar rehabilitation 1941-52	27.7	26.1	Plastics (25%) Organic chemistry technology (13%), Textile technology, traffic means & power (all 11%)	11
High growth period 1953-66	23.4	25.3	Traffic means & power (26%) Communication technology (16%) Plastics (13%) Civil engineering technology, nuclear technology (all 10%)	18

Note: A = average total years (year of invention in foreign countries — years of first industrialisation in Japan); B = besides A, when year of utilisation is known in case of year of industrialisation in Japan equivocal, difference between year of invention and year of utilisation is computed.
Source: M. Saito, 'Introduction of Foreign Technology', *The Developing Economies*, vol. 13, no. 2 (Tokyo, June 1975), pp. 170-1.

In the initial industrialisation period in Japan there was a rapid annual increase in the number of technological introductions until World War I, followed by a slowdown until World War II. After the war, it increased rapidly in the period of high growth.[115] (See Table 2.9.) This has raised the serious question as to whether Japan can ever rid itself of this policy of imitation. Ohkawa and Rosovsky wrote:

> There seems to be general agreement on the following points: in the 1950s and 1960s Japan lagged behind the technological leaders (primarily the United States and to a lesser extent W. Germany); since the middle 1960s this technological gap has been rapidly growing smaller; Japanese business is now making great efforts through increased research and development expenditures and similar devices to develop its own advanced technology.[116]

Has the gap, however, really been closing? The following evidence points to the contrary. Taking the sum of contracts for technology imported under the Foreign Capital Law and those under the Foreign Currency Trade Management Law, reveals an increasing trend for approved contracts — from 310 in 1956 to 2,403 in 1973; the number more than doubled between 1966 and 1972. Payments for foreign technology also increased rapidly from $147 million to $487 million between 1966 and 1972, nearly a threefold increase.[117]

One important casualty of technology transfer or imported industrialisation, in terms of its effects on cultural development, particularly in a period when technology has become increasingly sophisticated requiring less and less labour, has been individualism, the growth of which was, in European experience, functionally related to the process of industrialisation. In Japan (and most underdeveloped countries) people are less individualistic and are more oriented towards the needs of groups, including the family, pseudo-familial business enterprises and the state.

When economic development is based on imported technology and does not result from an industrial revolution it is often carried out by large-scale monopolies helped by the state. Free competitive forces provoked by the development of individualism are not dominant in such a development pattern. Education, which is also transplanted for obvious reasons, does not help the development of individualism; on the contrary, it frequently acts as a hindrance.

Japanese education, rather than putting the emphasis on originality and certainty, aims at having the pupil imitate his teacher – thus developing the capability to repeat as closely as possible what should be done. Obviously, to copy technology from overseas does not require any independent thinking. Learning by imitation does not help the development of individual initiative.

Dore calls this the 'late development effect' which has a conservative influence.[118] The fact that other developed countries already existed to serve as models meant that Japan could pick and choose, and did not need to work out any industrial technology or social technology, such as educational systems of her own. In Dore's view this has meant that the Japanese concentrate on adapting the details of imported technology and education to their own system rather than on devising major innovations of their own. This process results in the absence of desired learning-intensity, to use Hirschman's term.[119] This type of technological innovation has not resulted from man's association with his environment through the process of 'learning by doing' and thus does not help the growth of original thinking and individualism.

The question remains: will Japan become more individualistic with further modernisation? The answer is negative as long as Japan depends on imported technology as the basic force behind its process of modernisation, which it will have to go on doing, as shown in the section on industrial transplantation in Japan.

Other scholars, such as Nakane and Dore, have reached the same conclusion, although for different reasons.[120]

It is therefore said of Japanese development that Japan, an Asian nation, Westernised and subsequently modernised its society successfully to win today's economic prosperity. However, this Westernisation is only superficial, being a product of the imitation of Western technology in the process of development. This is equally true of the modern sectors of underdeveloped countries for the same reason. It has been rightly pointed out by an anthropologist of Kyoto University that Japan is not as Westernised as she may appear. Westernisation is only a facade, and the substance of Japanese civilisation has hardly changed after Japan's contact with the West.[121]

However there is some cultural influence in industrial latecomer countries where economic development without an industrial revolution is attempted. The same conclusion is also applicable to all underdeveloped countries where terms like 'Westernisation' and 'economic development' have become synonymous. However, we must mention that industrial latecomers of the early and mid-nineteenth century escaped this cultural influence due to the fact that the capital and technology that these countries imported from the country of classical industrial revolution were simple and highly labour-using, as the process of industrialisation was at its initial stage and the factor supply situation at that time favoured labour-intensive technology. Consequently, imports of technology at that time required the transfer of more and more labour from the agricultural sector, the largest sector of the economy, and therefore encouraged the mechanisation of agriculture. The expanding market for manufactured goods, the production of which was confined to a few countries, hastened this process of integration. This made these nineteenth-century latecomers work out their own industrial technology and social technology (such as educational systems) and thus developed their individualism and distinct cultural life. Japan missed such an integrated development, as discussed earlier.

Notes

1. J.R. Hicks, *A Theory of Economic History* (Oxford, 1969), p. 141.

2. F.F. Mendels, 'Proto-Industrialisation', *Journal of Economic History*, March no. 1, vol. 32 (1972), p. 240.

3. P. Bairoch, *The Economic Development of the Third World* (Methuen, London, 1973), pp. 203-4.

4. E.L. Jones (ed.), *Agriculture and Economic Growth in England, 1650-1815* (Methuen, London, 1967), p. 12.

5. A. Toynbee, *Lectures on the Industrial Revolution of the 18th Century in England* (New York), pp. 41-5.

6. Jones, *Agriculture*, p. 7.

7. Ibid., p. 8.

8. Bairoch, *Third World*, pp. 452-3.

9. Ibid., p. 453.

10. Ibid., pp. 453-4.

11. N. Tranter, *Population since the Industrial Revolution* (Croom Helm, London, 1973), pp. 63-93.

12. Bairoch, *Third World*, p. 490.

13. Ibid., p. 491.

14. Ibid., pp. 491-2.

15. Ibid.

16. Ibid., p. 453.

17. E.J.T. Collins, 'Labour Supply and Demand in European Agriculture, 1800-1880' in E.L. Jones and S.J. Woolf (eds.), *The Historical Role of Agrarian Change in Economic Development* (Methuen, London, 1969), p. 74.

18. E.J. Hobsbawm, *Industry and Empire* (Pelican, Harmondsworth, 1969), p. 39.

19. L.C.A. Knowles, *The Industrial and Commercial Revolution* (Routledge, London, 1930), pp. 76 ff.

20. Ibid., p. 77.

21. Ibid., p. 93.

22. S.B. Clough and R.T. Rapp, *European Economic History* (McGraw Hill, 1975), pp. 258-68.

23. Ibid., pp. 261-2.

24. D.N. McClosky, 'The Enclosure of Open Fields: Preface to the Study of its Impact on the Efficiency of English Agriculture in the Eighteenth Century', *Journal of Economic History*, voL 32, no. 1 (March 1972).

25. S.B. Clough and C.W. Cole, *The Mechanisation of Industry in the Economic History of Europe*, p. 423.

26. Clough and Rapp, *Economic History*, p. 263.

27. 'Just how essential these technical improvements were to the improvement of agriculture can be imagined when one realises that with oxen a farmer could turn over only about a third of an acre a day. With horses he could plough about twice this amount but the work was back-breaking, especially in stony ground where the ploughman might be thrown head over heels when the plough hit a stone. Harvesting with a sickle could proceed at about a fifth of an acre a day and with a scythe at a third of an acre.' Clough and Rapp, *Economic History*, pp. 264-5.

28. Bairoch, *Third World*, pp. 488-92; Clough and Rapp, *Economic History*, pp. 265-6.

29. Clough and Rapp, *Economic History*, pp. 272-84.

30. Hobsbawm, *Industry*, p. 98.

31. J. Gould, *Economic Growth in History* (Methuen, London, 1973), p. 107.

32. P. Deane and W.A. Cole, *British Economic Growth 1688-1959* (Cambridge University Press, 1962), p. 94.

33. Jones, *Agriculture*, pp. 12-15.

34. F.M.L. Thompson, 'The Social Distribution of Property in England since the sixteenth Century', *Economic History Review*, XIX (1966), pp. 505-17.

35. Jones, *Agriculture*, p. 14.

36. G.E. Mingey, *English Landed Society in the Eighteenth Century* (Routledge and Kegan Paul, London, 1963), p. 89.

37. Ibid., p. 183.

38. G.E. Mingey, 'The Size of Farms in the Eighteenth Century', *Economic History Review*, XIX (1966), pp. 480-1.

39. Jones, *Agriculture*, p. 18.

40. Average farm size at that time was 189 acres. See Mingey, 'Size of Farms', p. 481.

41. G.D.H. Cole, *Introduction to Economic History 1750-1950* (New York), p. 43.

42. Jones and Woolf, *Agrarian Change*, pp. 74-91.

43. Ibid., p. 76.

44. T.S. Ashton, *The Industrial Revolution 1760-1830* (Oxford, 1964), p. 44.

45. A. Redford, *Labour Migration in England* (Manchester University Press, London, 1926), p. 63.

46. J.R.D. Chambers, 'Enclosure and the Labour Supply in the Industrial Revolution' in Jones, *Agriculture*, pp. 95-100.

47. R.H. Tawney, *The Agrarian Problem in the Sixteenth Century* (Longmans, London, 1912), p. 109.

48. E.C.K. Gonner, *Common Land and Enclosures* (Macmillan, 1912), p. 441.

49. N. Riches, *Agrarian Revolution in Norfolk* (Chapel Hill, 1937), p. 95; Chambers, 'Enclosure', p. 98.

50. Arthur Young, 'Farmer's Tour through the East of England', *Annals of*

Agriculture (1770); Chambers, 'Enclosure', p. 100.

51. Adam Smith, *Wealth of Nations*, Book I, Ch. VIII.

52. F.M. Eden and T. Malthus, 'State of the Poor, 1797', *Essays on Population* (1798); Chambers, 'Enclosure'.

53. Chambers, 'Enclosure', pp. 81-94.

54. Jones, *Agriculture*, p. 22; Deane and Cole, *Economic Growth*, p. 143.

55. Jones, *Agriculture*, p. 24.

56. Ibid.

57. Arthur Young, 'Of Manufacturers Mixed with Agriculture', *Annals of Agriculture* (1799), p. 221.

58. S. Kuznets, 'Underdeveloped Countries and the Pre-Industrial Phase in the Advanced Countries', *Proceedings of the World Population Conference*, vol. V (1954).

59. Jones, *Agriculture*.

60. J. Hughes, *Industrialisation and Economic History* (McGraw Hill, 1970), p. 52.

61. Clough and Cole, *Mechanisation*, pp. 435-6.

62. S. Kuznets, *Industrial Distribution of National Product and Labour Force, Economic Development and Cultural Change*, vol. 6, no. 4 (July 1957), pp. 84, 88, 89 and 91.

63. Clough and Rapp, *Economic History*, p. 275.

64. P. Hohenberg, 'Changes in Rural France in the Period of Industrialisation, 1830-1940', *Journal of Economic History*, vol. 32 (1972), pp. 224-5.

65. Ibid., p. 225.

66. Ibid., p. 225.

67. Henry Louis, 'Population in France in the Eighteenth Century' in D.V. Glass and D.E.C. Eversly (eds.), *Population in History* (Arnold, London, 1965).

68. Hohenberg, 'Rural France', p. 224.

69. Ibid., p. 226.

70. Collins, 'Labour Supply'.

71. Hohenberg, 'Rural France', p. 228.

72. Ibid., p. 228.

73. Ibid., p. 230.

74. This trend has changed in recent times with the introduction of the Green Revolution approach. But as Green Revolution techniques are based on outside resources and are beyond the scope of the large majority of farmers, increase in investment in this respect has had little impact on the rural economy as a whole, in terms of creating more productive employment. It is true that modernisation in the name of the Green Revolution will throw resources out of agriculture to urban sectors. But there is a fly in the ointment, i.e. the urban sectors and modernisation techniques of agriculture are both based on foreign resources and technology and as a result, neither the urban sectors nor the supply of resources for modernising agriculture in the name of the Green Revolution are capable of creating a demand for labour. Hence the army of urban unemployed has been swelling at a much greater rate today than before. It has little to do with population growth. Agricultural revolution cannot be substituted by Green Revolution.

75. P. Bairoch, *Agriculture and the Industrial Revolution* (Fontana, London, 1969), p. 69.

76. E.J. Hobsbawm, *The Industrial Revolution in the Age of Revolution* (Weidenfeld and Nicolson, 1962), p. 31.

77. M. Kitchen, *The Political Economy of Germany 1815-1914* (Croom Helm, London, 1978), pp. 10-11.

78. Ibid., p. 62.

79. D.S. Landes, 'Industrialisation and Economic Development in Nineteenth

Century Germany', *First International Conference on Economic History* (Stockholm, August 1960), pp. 84-6; L.C.A. Knowles, *Economic Development in the 19th Century* (London, 1932), pp. 157-71.

80. Collins, 'Labour Supply', pp. 61-4.

81. See P. Dardel, *Holker, Guilband and Morris, 1752-9* (Rouen, 1942).

82. B. Grill, *Les Origines de la grande industrie metallurgique en France* (1947).

83. Arthur Young, who travelled in France from 1787-9 gave the following interesting account of the iron works of William Wilkinson in his Journal for 23 September 1788: 'Messrs. Epivent had the goodness to attend me in a water expedition, to view the establishment of Mr. Wilkinson, for boring cannon, in an island in the Loire below Nantes. Until that well known English manufacturer arrived, the French knew nothing of the art of casting cannon solid, and then boring them. Mr. Wilkinson's machinery, for boring four cannons, is now at work, moved by tide wheels; but they have erected a steam engine, with a new apparatus for boring seven more'. See B. Edwards (ed.), *Arthur Young's Travels in France* (Bell, London, 1905), p. 134.

84. At the end of the Napoleonic wars a number of French ironmasters and mining officials were sent to England to study modern methods of iron and steel production. In 1823 Wright's machine to make pins was imported to France; in 1826-9 a number of machines used in the manufacture of cloth were also imported. There are numerous examples of such imports to France in the nineteenth century. See W.O. Henderson, *Britain and Industrial Europe, 1750-1870* (Liverpool University Press, 1954), Chs. I and II.

85. Henderson, *Industrial Europe*, pp. 10-76.

86. W.O. Henderson, *The State and the Industrial Revolution in Prussia, 1740-1870* (Liverpool University Press, 1952).

87. Landes, 'Industrialisation', pp. 83-7.

88. Henderson, *Industrial Europe*, Chs. I and IV.

89. Henderson, *Industrial Europe* and *The State*; Hobsbawm, *Industry*.

90. Kitchen, *Economy of Germany*, p. 61.

91. E.S. Crawcour, 'The Japanese Economy on the Eve of Modernisation', *The Journal of Oriental Society in Australia*, vol. 2, no. 1 (June 1963), p. 37.

92. H. Rosovsky, 'Japan's Transition to Economic Growth, 1868-1885' in H. Rosovsky (ed.), *Industrialisation in Two Systems* (Wiley, 1966), p. 103.

93. It is, however, true that the density of population in Japan at the beginning of the Meiji Restoration was extremely high with 1.03 hectares of cultivated land per household compared with 10.57 hectares in England and Wales. But as population density is a static concept and population growth a dynamic one, it is more significant to use the population growth rate to study the development process. See I. Tauber, *The Population of Japan* (Princeton University Press), Chs. II and IV.

94. Rosovsky, 'Japan', p. 119.

95. See P. Maitra, *Underdevelopment Revisited* (Firma KLM, Calcutta, 1977), Ch. 3.

96. H. Otsuka, 'Modernisation Re-considered with special reference to Japan', *The Developing Economics*, vol. 3, no. 4 (December 1965), pp. 392-4.

97. K. Takahashi, *The Rise and Development of Japan's Modern Economy* (The JIJI Press, Tokyo, 1969), pp. 60-4, 110-13.

98. Ibid., pp. 10-89.

99. G.C. Allen, 'Japan's Economic Growth' in C.D. Cowan (ed.), *The Economic Development of China and Japan* (Allen and Unwin, London, 1964), p. 194.

100. S. Tobata, Foreword in R.P. Dore, *Reform in Japan* (Oxford University Press, London, 1959), p. ix.

101. T. Ogura (ed.), *Agricultural Development in Modern Japan* (Japan FAO

Organisation, Tokyo, 1963), p. 8.

102. R.P. Sinha, 'Japan's Early Economic Development', *Scottish Journal of Political Economy*, no. 16 (1969), p. 115.

103. Dore ¦ Land Reform in Japan (Oxford University Press, 1959), p. 17.

104. Ibid., p. 17.

105. W. McCord, 'The Japanese Model' in C.K. Wilber (ed.), *The Political Economy of Development and Underdevelopment* (Random House, New York, 1973), pp. 280-1.

106. P. Baran, *The Political Economy of Growth* (Monthly Review Press, New York, 1960); H. Rosovsky, *Capital Formation in Japan* (New York, 1961).

107. K. Ohkawa and H. Rosovsky, 'The Role of Agriculture in Modern Japanese Economic Growth', *Economic Development and Cultural Change*, part II (October 1960), p. 45.

108. J.I. Nakamura, *Agricultural Production and Economic Development in Japan* (Princeton University Press, 1966), pp. 119-53; T. Oshima, 'Notes on an Alternative Method of Estimating the National Income and Expenditure of Japan, 1881', *Keijai Kenkyn*, vol. 8, no. 3 (Hitotshubashi University, 1957), pp. 242-51; Sinha, 'Economic Development', pp. 112-14.

109. W. Kelly *et al.*, *Dualistic Economic Development* (University of Chicago, 1972), p. 158.

110. According to Nakamura, agricultural production was just keeping pace with population growth (which was 0.8 to 1.3 per cent until 1914). See Nakamura, *Agricultural Production*, pp. 119-22, 151.

111. G.C. Allen, *A Short Economic History of Japan* (Allen and Unwin, London, 1946), Table X, p. 120; Sinha, 'Economic Development'.

112. Sinha, 'Economic Development', pp. 112-14.

113. Ibid., pp. 121-2.

114. T. Blumenthal, 'The Catching-up Process as a Factor in Japan's Economic Growth', *International Symposium Paper* (L'Bocconi University, Milan, 1966), p. 2.

115. A recent Report of the Science and Technology Agency of the Government of Japan shows the enormous volume of technology Japan imports every year. According to this report, Japanese imports were $572 million for foreign-patented expertise in one fiscal year, 1972. More than 80 per cent of the so-called 'inventions' patented in Japan by Japanese 'inventors' between 1946 and 1965 were based on ideas and information gleaned from foreign (chiefly US) journals, magazines and catalogues, or were produced by breaking down the products used, shown off, sold or given away by GIs or War Department personnel in Japan. Not only technology, but sales management, accounting and auditing methods have all been borrowed from other countries. The Japanese process of industrialisation was initiated by imports of capital and technology from abroad (of course, earned against her primary exports) and the subsequent progress in industrialisation has been made by the importation of technology against her expanding exports of manufactures. See P. Maitra, 'Notes on Japan's Economic Miracle', *The Asian Economic Review*, 17, nos. 1-3 (1975), pp. 121-2.

116. K. Ohkawa and H. Rosovsky, *Japanese Economic Growth* (Stanford, 1973), p. 237.

117. K. Sato, 'Growth and Technical Change in Japan's Non-primary Economy, 1930-67', *Japanese Economic Studies* (Summer 1973), pp. 63-103.

118. Dore, *Reform in Japan*, p. 19.

119. A.O. Hirschman, 'Political Economy of Import Substitution', *Quarterly Journal of Economics*, vol. 82, no. 1 (February 1968), pp. 10-23.

120. C. Nakane, *Japanese Society* (Weidenfeld and Nicolson, London, 1970); R.P. Dore, *British Factory, Japanese Factory* (University of California, 1973), p. 12.

121. T. Umesao, 'Cultural Background of Japan's Economy', *The Japan Times* (Tokyo, December 1974).

122. Present-day Japan has been discussed in this light in P. Maitra, 'Japanese Pattern of Development Implications for the Third World', *NZ Asia Studies* (Auckland University, forthcoming).

3 TECHNOLOGY TRANSFER, POPULATION GROWTH, AND ECONOMIC DEVELOPMENT SINCE THE INDUSTRIAL REVOLUTION

In this chapter we have examined the nature of the 'population take-off' that occurred during the early period of industrialisation in the late eighteenth and early nineteenth centuries in England and in other parts of the Continent, (e.g. France and Germany) which helps in understanding the nature of the problems of population facing developing countries of the mid-twentieth century. In the following section a more detailed examination of technology transfer and its effects on resource utilisation has been attempted in the context of the above two questions.

The 'population take-off' or 'population revolution' in the late eighteenth and early nineteenth centuries played a vital role in the industrial revolution in England. An important study made by E. Boserup[1] points out that population pressure spurred agricultural revolution and led to the industrial revolution. (See Appendix.) Habakkuk[2] suggested that population took off because economic development necessitated a sharp increase in the size of the labour force, thereby encouraging people to marry earlier and have larger families even though there was no improvement in the real standard of living; in other words, the demand for labour encouraged a higher fertility rate. Tranter wrote while dealing with this period that the 'stimulus to fertility' brought about by increasing employment opportunities may have been a significant determinant of the 'population take-off in England'.[3]

At the initial period of the agricultural and industrial revolution changes in technique and production involved simple processes and required more labour for obvious reasons, and thus the vast increase in the demand for adult and child labour encouraged earlier marriage and higher rates of marital fertility by raising the average level of money (though not real) incomes. This latter aspect (i.e. higher money wages than real) played a very important role in determining the levels of employment of an increasing supply of labour in the classical model of macro-economics and economic development. However, with the high pace of development, technology became more and more sophisticated. Thus the need for relatively skilled labour. This made child labour unnecessary, and led to the introduction of compulsory education. This made children expensive, which acted as a disincentive towards high

70

fertility and thus the fertility rate began to drop, particularly from the early twentieth century. But increase in the demand for labour (as a stimulus to the fertility rate) as an explanation of the population explosion in other parts of Europe has been questioned by many authors. It cannot be regarded as the common denominator which shaped the demographic experience of all Western European countries in the late nineteenth century.[4] In contemporary France the primary mechanism at work seems to be declining mortality rather than rising fertility as was the case with England. Tranter is right in suggesting that we must look at those developments which might have led to a reduction in the general level of mortality.[5] But in his diagnosis of 'those developments' he has missed a very vital economic factor that distinguishes the pattern of industrialisation in England from that in other parts of contemporary Europe, which largely explains the fact that the population take-off in Europe was more influenced by the decreasing mortality rates than by the increasing fertility rates.

According to Drake[6] and Tranter[7], one possible cause of a decline in mortality rates might have been the widespread adoption of certain improvements in medical practice. The two best documented possibilities are (i) the spread of better hospital facilities and (ii) the introduction of inoculation and vaccination against smallpox. According to Tranter, 'population take-off in many West European countries no doubt owed something to these innovations. But they cannot be considered as the sole, or even the principal reasons for the increase in rates of population growth'.[8]

Another explanation suggested by many authors regarding the increase in rates of population growth in the various countries of Western Europe during the late eighteenth and early nineteenth centuries may after all have simply been the result of a quite fortuitous natural reduction in the severity of epidemic disease. This might be due to a reduction in the strength of epidemic viruses or an increase in the resistance of the human host toward such viruses. Better economic opportunities, changed ways of life and increased availability of food must have been important in the increased resistance of the human host. All available statistics of the period show that, in England, population took off earlier and increased more dramatically than in most other areas because of the stimulus exerted by industrialisation (working through higher fertility, inoculation and vaccination, the use of new drugs and the spread of improved hospital facilities, which might also be explained as results of a general improve-ment in economic productivity). In France (and, for that matter, other Western European countries), on the other hand, the relatively small upturn in the rate of population growth in the late eighteenth and early nineteenth centuries was due to the deliberate limitation of marital fertility by large sections of the French population.

One important factor that explains this divergence in the pattern of population growth between England, France and other Western European nations is traceable to differences in the process of industrialisation as mentioned earlier. This vital factor needs serious consideration.

In England, economic growth was characterised by the rapid and simultaneous development of all three main branches of the economy — agriculture, industry and commerce, as a result of the process of the industrial revolution.[9] Obviously, this process had a great impact in terms of demand for labour. It has been concluded by many economic historians that there is no doubt that the modest but quite definite up-turn in the pace of economic activity in England after 1750 was largely due to the simultaneous increase in rates of population growth.

Professor J.D. Chambers in his 'The Vale of Trent, 1670-1800' showed how an increasing population prepared the way for economic advance by easing the problems previously caused by the labour shortage. He wrote: 'to the innovators of the sixties and seventies the labour force which had been conspicuous by its scarcity and truculence in the forties was no longer an obstacle to change; it was both more plentiful and was becoming more amenable'.[10] However, France and Germany, for example, followed the process of imported industrialisation from England, the nation of the first Industrial Revolution. Paul Bairoch pointed out this difference in terms of the growth of the iron and steel industry in England to meet the growing need of the agricultural economy, whereas in France and Germany, the iron and steel industries owed their origin to the needs of railways, shipbuilding and consumer goods industries.[11] Imported capital and skills from England played the initial role in the development of industries on the Continent. Consequently, unlike in England, simultaneous development of all three sectors of the economy did not take place.[12] It is more or less an accepted fact today that the English played an important part in the industrialisation of Western Europe. W.O. Henderson summarised the ways in which England acted as a pioneer of industrialisation on the Continent. Firstly, skilled British workers installed new machinery and then instructed foreign workers how to use it. Thus in the second half of the eighteenth century British textile workers were teaching the French how to use the fly-shuttle, the water-frame and the mule jenny, while British engineers installed steam pumps and other machinery. In the second quarter of the nineteenth century, groups of English puddlers moved from one iron works to another in Belgium and Germany instructing the locals in their craft. A little later an English driver on the footplate of a locomotive was as familiar a figure on the Continent as an English marine engineer on a river steamboat or an English foreman in a cotton mill. Secondly, for fifty years or so after the Napoleonic wars, British companies borrowed some of the money necessary to start important industrial enterprises on the Continent. Railway companies, river navigation companies, gasworks, waterworks, cotton and other textile mills and engineering establishments were set up with the aid of British capital. The development of the French textile industry owed much to British capital and technology. This is equally applicable to other industrialising countries of contemporary Europe.[13]

A huge volume of capital was transferred from England to France, Germany and other parts of the Continent. Britain supplied entrepreneurs and managers who formed and managed modern industries there.

The implication of England supplying capital and skills to the Continent for our present analysis is that employment effects of industrialisation in Western European countries were much less than in England and thus were not as great a stimulus to fertility as in England. Population, undoubtedly, was growing fast in Europe, but largely due to the fall in mortality rates resulting from factors mentioned before, which were also largely imported from England. Because technology was simple at the initial stage of the industrial revolution, imported industrialisation at that time was labour-intensive which was sufficient to absorb this population growth. However, the evidence shows that initially these economies had to face a dualistic structure, composed of a modern industrial sector on the one hand and a labour surplus rural sector on the other.

If we take the English as a guide, because the first Industrial Revolution initiating modern development occurred in England (we have noted the differences of the English experience with respect to other European countries), the effect of economic development on long-term variations in the level of human fertility appears to vary according to the particular stage of economic development concerned. Thus in the late eighteenth and early nineteenth centuries, the initial growth of the industrial economy acted as a positive stimulus to earlier marriage and higher rates of marital fertility; it did so because of the enormous opportunities it offered for child labour.[14] This is the first stage and happened only in England.

Certain key influences affected the supply of labour. These included the laws relative to child labour, the reduction in child and infant mortality, the introduction of old age pensions, widening opportunities for female employment, new and optimistic attitudes towards material standards of living and the skill requirements of new and sophisticated technologies. These factors combined to reduce the birth rate. We must add here that the impact of the 'keeping up with the Jones' attitude, produced and nurtured in developed capitalist economies, has also played a forceful role in keeping fertility rates down.[15]

High rates of population growth from the mid-eighteenth to the early twentieth centuries were associated with, and particularly responsible for, industrial 'take-off' and sustained rapid economic advance. Underdeveloped countries are unfortunate to have missed the beneficial effects of industrialisation and also the demand for labour which is normally created in this process of industrialisation. Rapid population growth in underdeveloped countries has been mainly due to a steady fall in mortality rate. Despite the growth of industries which brought about a remarkable growth in output, these countries face ever increasing problems of population and poverty. It may be termed 'population inflation', unlike the population take-off of the nineteenth century, as the population growth in underdeveloped countries has not been accompanied by the growth of productivity. It is difficult to see whether recent attempts in some countries to bring about a reduction in the birth rate through compulsory birth control measures will have the desired effect. They will rather lead to a population structure burdened with ageing people with skills and education unsuitable for the ever growing technology available from abroad. Leibenstein pointed this out, although from a different angle. He wrote explaining the term 'quality replacement effect': 'By this I have in mind that if the entrants to a labour force have acquired more skill and education than those who leave it, then other things being equal, the greater the entry, the better. At least temporarily, as the average acquired qualities of the population, improve more rapidly, the greater the population growth.'[16]

When we look at underdeveloped countries in the mid-twentieth century trying to industrialise, we notice a different picture. In this world the birth rate has been more or less constant in effect, with a falling rate in urban areas and a rising or a constant rate in rural areas, and, in some cases, there is a declining trend; on the other hand, the death rate has shown a down turn due to the availability of modern medical technology and foreign aid etc., reducing the incidence of epidemics and famines. Obviously, the fall in mortality rates has very little to do with the national income and economic activities of these countries. In other words, industrialisation of these countries is essentially based on sophisticated capital and technology and resources available through foreign aid, trade, investment by multinational corporations etc. It has created, on the one hand, little demand for labour and on the other, opportunities, although very limited, for a sophisticated living, both acting as a disincentive to high marital fertility and nuptiality in urban areas. But this tendency is limited to the modern sector that comprises only ten to twelve per cent of the total population. In the large traditional sector or subsistence sector the labour surplus produces an attitude of indifference, or acts as an incentive towards a larger family as it is economically advantageous due to the factor endowment situations and level of economic activity prevailing in this sector, and because of the social security role (for example, old age pensions, unemployment benefit etc.) of large families.

The modern and industrialising sectors of these countries, because of the pattern of investment, have led these economies to skip over the first demographic effects of industrialisation. The stage of creating demand for labour and thereby absorbing surplus labour did not materialise. In the case of France and Germany, the process of industrialisation, initially based on imported technology and capital, did not create a stimulus to fertility but created opportunities of employment for the growing population resulting from declining mortality rates. The reason, stated before, was that the technology and capital that France and Germany imported was simple and labour-intensive enough to absorb the growing population resulting from the fall in mortality but obviously it could not create the same demand for labour as the industrial revolution did in England. What were the effects of transfers of manufactured goods, capital and technology from developed to underdeveloped countries since the industrial revolution? They led to de-industrialisation but with a fundamental difference from that in Europe.

Daniel Thorner who investigated the alleged phenomenon of the de-industrialisation of India as a result of contacts with the industrialisation of England in the nineteenth century came to the conclusion that there can be no dispute with the statement that India's national handicrafts have declined slowly from their former glory. This falling-off, however, was not a phenomenon peculiar to India but a worldwide development affecting different countries at different times. The skill, sooner or later, of the old-style craftsman was as integral a part of the industrial revolution as the coming of the factory system.[17] His conclusion is a result of a serious omission to take into account the vital point of difference in the process of industrialisation in the UK and other European countries, and the colonies.

In Britain it was her own industrial revolution which led to the destruction of handicrafts so that employment was being created in one branch of secondary industry while it was shrinking in another; after a point, the rate of creation of employment in the new branch of secondary industry was far higher than the rate of loss in the other branch. The same process worked in other parts of the Continent, although with some differences as discussed before. The impact of industrialisation in the West on employment and income in the secondary industries of today's underdeveloped countries was almost entirely destructive. The reason has been aptly pointed out by John Hicks who wrote: 'The English handloom weavers, who were displaced by textile machinery could (in the end and after much travail) find re-employment in England; but what of the Indian weavers who were displaced by the same improvement? Even in their case there would be a favourable effect, somewhere but it might be anywhere; there would be no particular reason why it should be in India. The most likely is that it will suffer long lasting damage now and then, from a backlash of improvements that have occurred elsewhere.'[18]

Population Dependent on Secondary Industry in Gangetic Bihar, 1809-13 and 1901[19]

	Industrial Population	Percentage of Industrial to total Population
Around 1809-13	1,316,776	18.6
1901	987,752	8.5

According to another estimate for the Bengal area, taking cotton weavers, cotton growers, spinners, dressers, embroidery etc. together, one million people in Bengal (including Bihar and Orissa) were thrown out of employment by 1828.[20]

The Bengal Chamber of Commerce complained to the Government of India in the early 1860s that the demand for English cotton goods in the north western provinces had fallen off and that this was due to the arrival of handloom weaving. The Government had an extensive enquiry instituted into the facts of the case and the secretary of the Sudhar Board of Revenue summarised the most important finding in the following words:

First, that it may be stated decidedly that the diminished demand for English cotton has not been caused by increased Native

manufacture. With few exceptions there has been nowhere any such
increase. On the contrary, there has, speaking generally, been a marked
and distressing contraction of local manufactures. This is less desirable
in the western districts, where perhaps from a sixth to a fourth of the
looms in the cities and towns (though not in the outlying villages)
have stopped working. But in the eastern districts the trade has altogether decayed, and within two or three years the falling off is
shown to have reached a third, and in some districts, a half of the
looms, even of the remainder a large portion is only worked occasion-
ally. The weavers have re-taken themselves to agricultural or other
menial labour, to menial service, emigration to the Mauritius and
elsewhere, and even to begging.[21]

In his well known work, *Conditions of Economic Progress*, Colin
Clark has presented a table to show that from 1881 to 1911 the proportion of the working force engaged in 'manufacturing, and construction', fell by half from 35 per cent to 17 per cent.[22]

In other words, the introduction of Western industrialisation in terms
of goods, capital, skill and technology in these countries instead of creating demand for labour, reduced it. The same process of industrialisation
is being followed now with the result that these economies are becoming increasingly incapable of solving the so-called overpopulation problem
despite the massive growth of modern sophisticated industries.

In some underdeveloped countries a vigorous programme of family
planning has been undertaken as a part of the programme for development.
Before we examine this point, we must note that family planning or birth
control was practiced in pre-industrial days in most societies, including
India. But it was adopted at the time of crop failures due to various
natural calamities, and not as a means to achieve economic development.
Population growth was conditioned by the harvest and epidemics in
those days. We noticed that at the time of the industrial revolution the
demand for labour created a stimulus to fertility but, when industrialisation in the developed capitalist world had gone a long way and was
capable of creating unending material advancements and a sophisticated
and secure living (at whose expense? – that is a different story), the
intense desire of individuals to ensure material advancement forced birth
rates down. This desire has resulted in the research, production, and
distribution of various methods of contraception. In other words, population control has never been associated with attempts to initiate economic development, i.e. at the take-off stage.

The danger of a policy of forced population control is that if it is successful (although that is very unlikely), it results in an increasing proportion of older people with fewer and fewer skills compatible with the technology that is transferred from the highly sophisticated economies. This danger of a high proportion of old people is becoming a reality already in developed economies where birth rates have shown a secular declining trend.

Technology Transfer

We have to delve into the past as well as go deeper into the phenomenon mentioned earlier to do justice to the above questions. It is a well known fact of history that there was a great deal of technology transfer from East to West in the past. During the pre-industrial days this transfer did not create any dualism in the West, and by using this technology the West produced modern science and technology. It must be noted that when Europe absorbed new ideas from outside, it did not do so in a purely passive and imitative manner, but often adapted them to local conditions or to new uses with distinct elements of originality. For example, the adoption of windmills that originally came from Persia, and the adoption of gunpowder from China. Professor Singer in his elaborate study of the history of technology observes that up to the sixteenth century the Near East was superior to the West in skill and inventiveness and the Far East was perhaps superior to both.[23] There were extensive branches of knowledge in which the West long and openly held the East as its master and instructor. The best products available to the West came from the East, whereas the West had little to offer to the East.[24]

The Europeans learned to use the compass from the Arabs, who also taught them how to distil alcohol.

Europe adapted new ideas from outside to local conditions or to new uses with distinctive elements of originality. The Persian windmill was built with a verticle axis. The windmill that spread throughout Europe, with great sails and a horizontal axis, was a much more efficient machine than the original conceived by the Persians. The Chinese invented gunpowder which they mostly used for fireworks while the Europeans adopted it for use in firearms. The Chinese invented paper and its manufacture spread to the Muslim Empire during the eight century. The Europeans learned the technique during the thirteenth century when the establishment of the first factories at Xativa and at Fabriano represented the transplanting into Europe of an idea born elsewhere.[25] One interesting point to note here is that while production of paper outside Europe was a manual process, in Europe the pulp was processed by machines driven by water mills. This may be taken as one of the proofs of the contention that the factor endowment situation, history and natural resources were the principal determinants of technology. This is also true of the present. Printing was invented by the Chinese, but in the West it was developed into an extremely efficient mass production process by the end of the fifteenth century.

Western technological development after the twelfth century was characterised by the increasing stress on mechanical aspects of technology. It has been argued that the harsher climate and environment, and the shortage of labour brought about by repeated epidemics favoured the adoption of labour-saving devices. The mechanical clock is considered as the original product of European invention in the twelfth century. It has been argued that the invention of the mechanical clock came in response to the European climate because during the winter the water in the clepsydras froze and the clouds all too often rendered the sundials useless. An interesting account was given in *Annali*, vol. I (p. 248), about the use of a machine to replace labour in the early fifteenth century. In 1402 the managers of the Fabbrica del Duomo in Milan studied the proposals for a stone-cutting machine which with the help of a horse (costing three shillings a day), would do the work for which four men (at a wage of 13 shillings per man per day) would otherwise be paid.

We may summarise the problem of technology transfer with respect to the labour surplus of the Third World countries of today with a sentence from P.E. Walker who wrote: 'Before men could evolve and apply the machine as a social phenomenon they had to become mechanics'.[26]

Technology transfer today is depriving the Third World countries of opportunities to become mechanics themselves and hence they have the perpetual problems of overpopulation, and social and cultural underdevelopment. One example of the flow of technology from East to West was the migration of the silk industry, which included not only the raw silk but also the technique of cultivation, as well as the mechanical contrivances required for the manufacture of silk goods. More important examples of technology transfer to the West were the introduction of gunpowder, which totally transformed military technology; the magnetic compass; the sternpost rudder; the fore and aft rig and other nautical innovations which revolutionised navigation; the rotary reel and spindle used for spinning; deep drilling which had profound effects on mining; paper making and printing; techniques in industrial chemistry and building construction; and the Arabic (originally Indian) system of numerals, the adoption of which made an immense contribution to the rise of science. The windmill appeared first in Persia in the seventh century. The spinning wheel was known in China in the eleventh century, more than one hundred years before it first appeared in Europe. Professor Benedict wrote:

> Perhaps we describe this civilisation as built on steel and gunpowder. But steel was invented in India or in Turkistan and gunpowder in China. Perhaps we prefer to identify our Western culture by its printing press and literature but paper and printing were both borrowed from China. Our control of nature is overwhelmingly dependent on mathematical calculations. But the so-called Arabic system of notations which is essential to all complicated mathematics was unknown in Europe in the Roman era; it was invented in Asia and introduced to our civilisation by the Moors. Algebra was a method of calculation also borrowed by Europeans from Asiatic peoples.[27]

The Mayans and the Khmers produced tropical civilisations as architecturally elaborate as those of the ancient Mediterranean. Tropical Africa has had a great continuous artistic tradition and the more we know of even what used to be thought of as primitive societies, the more complex and remarkable their achievements become.[28] The whole course of human history shows that many tropical societies have achieved complex social structures, great architecture and art and that human organisation and learning capacity have been able to overcome in many instances the unfavourable aspects of climate. It is to be noted here that these unfavourable aspects of climate were not as harsh as in the West, where it required greater exertions of human intellect and effort just to eke out a living. Thus in the sixteenth century the civilisation of Northern India was certainly as advanced technologically and artistically as that of Europe. It has also been pointed out by scholars that yield per man and yield per unit of land were higher in India than in the more progressive of the West European countries in the seventeenth century. Comparisons of the seed/yield ratio for individual crops were also more favourable for India. India had larger and richer urban areas than Europe before the industrial revolution.[29]

In the pre-industrial epoch, production techniques and technology embodied the gradual accumulation of empirical knowledge, handed down from generation to generation through apprenticeship in the skilled trades. In this process some changes in techniques took place to suit the needs of the time and place. But the techniques were simple and labour-intensive for obvious reasons. The productive activity gave rise to further productive activity, just as one generation gives birth to the next. In the East, because of the favourable climatic conditions, and resources provided by nature, this simple process of technological change was considered sufficient to provide the people with a simple living. Pressure of population was not high, death rate cancelling out birth rate. Although accurate information is not available, the most probable estimate seems to be that before their contact with the West many underdeveloped countries in Asia and Africa had high birth rates of almost four per cent.[30] In some parts of Africa and Latin America, slavery, and Portuguese and Spanish colonisation respectively led to depopulation which had a serious impact on their prevailing technology. In other words, resources provided by nature and manipulated by the prevailing simple technology were proved sufficient to maintain the people in a simple way of life. The congenial climate was an important factor in the continuation of the same economic, social and political system which was, however, always oppressive to the masses, whereas in the West a very harsh and uncongenial climate forced the people to improve upon the productive techniques as required by the growing volume of population.[31]

We should refer to Marx's writing on this. Marx wrote:

> It is not true that the most fruitful soil is the most fitted for the growth of the capitalist mode of production. This mode is based on the dominion of man over nature. Where nature is too lavish, she keeps him in hand, like a child in leading strings. She does not impose upon him any necessity to develop himself. It is not the tropics with their luxuriant vegetation, but the temperate zone, that is the Mother Country of Capital. It is not the mere fertility of the soil, but the differentiation of the soil, the variety of its natural products, the changes of the seasons, which form the physical basis for the social division of labour, and which, by changes in the natural surroundings, spur man on to the multiplication of his wants, his capabilities, his means and modes of labour. It is the necessity of bringing a natural force under the control of Society, of economising, of appropriating or subduing it on a large scale by the work of man's hand, that first plays the decisive part in the history of industry.[32]

One important question has troubled economic historians and development economists: why have not technically advanced and physically productive agricultures like those in the Middle East, China, and meso-America failed to bring about sustained growth, leading to an industrial economy? E.L. Jones and S.J. Woolf wrote in their important work, *The Historical Role of Agrarian Change in Economic Development*:

> Technically their farming organisation was superb, especially in the wet-rice areas where extensive irrigation networks were dug by 'covers' so large and well drilled as to make the problems of labour management in the early factory system look trifling. Equally, the physical volume of grain they produced was impressive. Yet their social histories were appalling tales of population cycles without a lasting rise in real incomes for the mass of the people on either the upswings or downswings. Their political histories are cycles of Cathay, the saga of dynasty after dynasty interrupted only by conquests or palace revolution which resulted in the retirement of one ruling clique by another. Why are these early agrarian empires essentially so sterile?[33]

It is evident from the history of these empires with immense state power, that their great agricultural works, which were undertaken to add new cultivatable land by the construction of irrigation canals, did not fundamentally change the system. We may mention the case of the Chinese Great Wall, 24 feet high studded by watch towers 500 yards apart at the most and so long that it would enclose large parts of France, Italy, Austria, Switzerland, Hungary, Rumania, Bulgaria, Poland and a segment of Russia.[34]

'Enormous resources of surveying and engineering skills, construction materials, labour and food (brought up for the workforce from riverine China) were expended on this.'[35] Alongside this type of expenditure of energy, the bureaucratic empires were concerned to glorify their rulers in a visible manner by the construction of palaces and tombs, such as the Pyramids or the Taj Mahal. The mass of the people, the agricultural peasantry, supplied the resources in the form of taxes and labour for public works which were unproductive in economic terms. These huge resources were used not to raise productivity but to satisfy the consumer demand of the aristocracy. Therefore these highly impressive archaeological constructions did not lead to commercialism or industrialisation.

The chances that the peasantry might raise their standard of living significantly and thus provide a broadly based market were severely circumscribed. Tax burdens were so onerous and collection was so efficient that local consumption was kept at a low, often a subsistence

level, and might be further depressed in times of stress. Any significant rise in the surplus of food produced above the subsistence level
could be skimmed off by the state. Consumer goods of any variety
were inevitably only available as luxury items. On the other hand,
labour for food production on the family holding and to meet
obligations to the state was a real asset. Probably this situation
might have encouraged population growth to meet whatever level of
food supplies could be produced and retained by the bulk of the
people.[36]

Some changes in agricultural practices such as new cropping patterns
or the introduction of new crops (like the introduction of the potato in
China or the medieval introduction of fast-ripening rice) might have
raised per capita income, stimulating growth which neutralised the rise
in per capita income. Besides, this increase in output would be mopped
up by taxation to provide for those magnificent constructions. Thus
'this response of static expansion whereby the agricultural base came to
support more people without an increase in income per head—was the
common historical experience of the pre-industrial world'.[37]

The case of medieval India, mentioned elsewhere, exemplifies this
point. The division of labour, and the diffusion of artisan skills, is
limited by the extent of the market which is again limited by the level
of productivity of the economy.

In the eighteenth and nineteenth centuries in England, the increased
pressure of population[38] forced changes in agrarian technology and
economic organisation, the former in the shape of the substitution of
wooden ploughs by iron ploughs and then steel ploughs. Thus the birth
of the iron and steel industry, the first pillar of modern industrial technology, owed its origin to agriculture in the UK. The history of
industrial change in France, Germany, USA etc. is different from the
UK as mentioned in Chapter I.[39]

However, in the nineteenth century, in England and other European
countries, rapid population growth was accompanied by a more rapid
growth in income resulting from the expansion of modern industrialisation which was helped by the effects of a cunningly propagated theory
of the international division of labour. Since the late nineteenth century,
the rapid growth of technology based on modern science to meet the
fast growing needs of international trade enabled these economies to
substitute labour, the supply of which was not keeping pace with the
economic growth rate due to the effects on fertility.[40] The result was
the rapid growth of income and a high standard of living in the industrial-

ised countries of the West. Why has this rapid growth of the industrialised countries failed to transmit its effects to the present day poor
nations? In other words, why has the international division of labour
failed in its objective of achieving mutual development? These questions
need careful discussion. It is tempting to assume with the mercantilists
that the enrichment of one community inevitably meant the impoverishment of the other. Because of the impact of the theory of the international division of labour followed in practice since the 1820s by the
few industrialised countries of the West, the mercantile character of
trade has not changed.[41] The prime force behind industrialisation in
latecomer countries today has been foreign trade, or imported industrialisation.

There is no denying the fact that since the nineteenth century there
has been a considerable transfer of technology, and in particular since
the 1950s, but this time from the West to the East, and accompanied by
an increasing gap between the two. This, however, did not happen when
technology was transferred from the East to the West in pre-industrial
days.

With the growing importance of an equipment industry based on
advanced technology, the situation was radically altered. Technology
transmission took the form of a straightforward commercial transaction,
and it became possible to transfer an entire productive sector at an unprecedented speed. England did this first by developing a transport equipment
industry, which transformed the means of transport throughout the world.
Further, by providing adequate financing for this industry it created a
mechanism for exporting capital which was to be a decisive factor in
the shaping of the world economic and social systems, commonly known
as the process of Westernisation.

The result was the growth and integration of the world economy in
the nineteenth century and the intensification of international special-
isation based on the international division of labour. It resulted in the
emergence of a few industrialised countries with rapidly rising incomes,
on the one hand, and on the other, a large number of primary producing
countries with a stagnating economy and income. World trade expanded
rapidly; but the external trade of underdeveloped countries was confined to those primary products which were needed by the economies of
the industrial centres, and investments in their production in underdeveloped countries were financed by them. In other words, the external
trade sector (e.g. jute, cotton, rubber, tin, cocoa etc.) which, in due course,
formed the modern sector in these countries, did not evolve to meet the
needs of the indigenous economies. To serve the purpose of these sectors

cities and towns were established, by-passing the existing indigenous urban centres that had evolved with the needs of the local economy.

Natural Resources and their Role

In this connection a brief reference may be made to the role of natural resources in economic development. We term those resources as natural because they are needed as raw material inputs in the process of industrialisation since the industrial revolution. Obviously, industrialisation as confined to Western countries has determined the nature and requirements of natural resources. Most suppliers of these natural resources have had nothing to do with them in terms of the needs of their economies at the time the cultivation, mining, plantation, or extraction of these resources was undertaken. Take for example rubber from Malaysia, or oil from the Middle East or for that matter copper or coffee from Africa.

There has been a tremendous increase in the output of extractive industries (see Table 3.1) in the countries of the Third World since the nineteenth century, but it was in no way due to the demand of local industry, indeed local industries absorbed only a fraction of production.

Table 3.1:   Index of Output of Extractive Industries of all Non-communist Less-Developed Countries

Year	Fuel	Minerals	(1963=100) All
1900	0.9	9.1	1.8
1913	3.3	17.9	4.8
1926-8	8.3	30.6	10.6
1936-8	12.4	37.8	15.1
1948	25.2	37.6	26.5
1953-5	45.1	56.1	46.2
1958-60	69.8	79.3	70.8
1963-5	108.2	106.3	108.0
1968-70	173.0	128.0	162.3

Source: P. Bairoch, *The Economic Development of the Third World* (Methuen, London, 1973), p. 53.

We can realise this if we compare output with exports of the products of mining and extraction. Thus for countries like Brazil, Chile, Liberia and Malaysia, exports of iron ore vary from 80 per cent to 100 per cent of production.[42] While in 1970 the underdeveloped countries produced 39 per cent of the world output of iron ore, the same countries produced slightly less than five per cent of the world's steel. Thus some 90 per cent of the iron ore mined in the underdeveloped countries goes to feed the blast furnaces of the developed countries. Now there is a paradox here, i.e. if these underdeveloped economies tried to utilise these resources themselves they would need highly capital-intensive technology which obviously would have to be imported. This implies that their indigenous human resources are to remain perpetually unemployed.[43]

If we look at the other end of the scale we find, for example, that between 1952 and 1970 the French iron and steel industries increased their processing of iron ore by about 2,700 per cent. Imports by all EEC countries of iron ore originating in the underdeveloped countries rose from 15 million tons in 1960 to 47 million tons in 1970.

These arguments are equally applicable to the nature of the natural resources of underdeveloped countries. This appears paradoxical when we notice that the so-called natural resources have very little to do with local economies. The type of natural resources and their discovery have been determined by the needs of the industrialised countries and thus many natural resources, because of the need for a rapid growth rate in manufacturing (which is confined to only 20 per cent of all nations of the world supplying 95 per cent of the products with a declining population growth rate), have lost their importance as raw materials in the process of production. For example, the use of coal as a source of energy has been increasingly replaced by oil in recent times. The case of cotton may also be referred to. Underdeveloped countries abound with surplus labour, the original source of energy, but it remains unutilised in a process of industrialisation based on technology and capital supplied by labour-short economies.

Table 3.2 shows that the provision of natural resources by UDCs has meant nothing to these countries in terms of development. It makes it extremely difficult to accept the view that, as countries like Tonga, Western Samoa etc. do not possess these natural resources required for the type of industrialisation we are familiar with, they cannot develop their economies without foreign assistance.

Conclusion

In summary, this description of the pattern of investment and industrialisation in underdeveloped countries as based on foreign capital and/or technology answers the two questions raised earlier: i.e. (i) Why has not the pressure of population led to economic development as it did in

Europe in the eighteenth and nineteenth centuries? (ii) Why has the technology transfer in modern times had an effect that is fundamentally different from the one that took place in the pre-industrial days, from the East to the West?

Table 3.2:   Changes in the Less-developed Countries' Share in World Production of Some Extractive Commodities, 1913-70 (in 1000s of Tons)

	1913	1928	1948	1960	1970
Iron Ore					
(FE Content)					
World production[1]	158,000[2]	73,000	87,300	172,300	285,000
Less-developed countries' output	4,000[2]	4,900	7,300	49,500	112,000
As % of total	3%	7%	8%	29%	39%
Bauxite					
World production[1]	550	2,100	8,400	25,100	53,500
Less-developed countries' output	2	450	5,100	17,000	31,800
As % of total	0.4%	21%	61%	68%	59%
Crude Petroleum					
World production[1]	44,800	171,000	438,000	901,000	1,964,000
Less-developed countries' output	6,900	43,000	156,000	497,000	1,314,000
As % of total	15%	25%	36%	55%	67%

Notes: 1. Excluding China and the USSR.
          2. Weight of ore and not iron content.
Sources: derived from various numbers of *Statistical Yearbook* (League of Nations); *Statistical Yearbook* (UN); *Eisen und Stahlstatistik* and *Petroleum Press Service*. (cf. Bairoch, P.).

The first problem arises from the fact that the population pressure has not spurred the introduction of agricultural innovations resulting in industrialisation i.e. more productive utilisation of indigenous resources has not resulted from the pressure of population as supported by history and observed by many economists. The basic reason is that the pattern of investment took the form of the transfer of resources and productivity in terms of capital, technology, skills and consumer goods which for obvious reasons did not require more productive utilisation of indigenous resources, and nor did the pattern of investment meet the needs of the growing pressure of population on the indigenous resources and technology. As a result the modern sector has grown in output, but because of its nature has absorbed fewer indigenous resources, and is surrounded by an indigenous sector that is stagnating but enlarging with growing population. In this pattern of investment this cannot be escaped. Since the start of the development decade, the same pattern and approach, with a difference only of degree, and not kind, has been followed and the same inevitable process of growth, as an island of sophistication surrounded by an expanding sea of poverty, has been continuing. And the gap between rich and poor, both internally and internationally, has been growing.

The second problem is related to differences of response to technology transfer in the pre-industrial and post-industrial periods and may be explained by the fact that in pre-industrial days the technology transferred from the East to the West was for obvious reasons highly labour-intensive and simple. Naturally the West, while absorbing technologies from the East, had to use indigenous resources and thus made possible the more productive use of these resources, through adapting these technologies to suit their own countries. This is true also of the process of industrialisation in France, Germany etc. which took place in the early period of the Industrial Revolution in England. These latecomer countries of the nineteenth century imported capital and technology from the country of Industrial Revolution which was relatively labour-intensive and thus helped create increasing opportunities for the more productive utilisation of indigenous resources. Therefore, the modern sector in these countries, though based on imported technology and capital, in its process of expansion and growth led to the gradual integration of the modern and traditional sectors and helped in the growth of a distinct indigenous culture and society and not their Anglicisation.[44] This process of rapid growth was also helped largely by the rapid expansion of international trade at the time which favoured most of the industrialising countries.

In the underdeveloped countries of today, the situation in this respect is basically different. The technology, capital and skill transferred from the West to these countries is highly sophisticated and capital-intensive, being a result of rapid economic growth and a declining population growth rate in a capitalist economic system. This transfer has undoubtedly resulted in a very rapid growth in the production of sophisticated goods and in the capital intensity of production but has not led to the more productive utilisation of domestic labour resources. That is why the indigenous cultures of these developing countries have not evolved since the nineteenth century and have become antique. The process of Westernisation has become a trend among the small segment of the total population belonging to the implanted 'modern sector'.

Industrialisation as the technique of using indigenous resources more productively, which results from man's association with his own environment, leads to the development of indigenous processes of production, and this forms the basic force behind the growth and evolution of an indigenous culture. The case of the classical Industrial Revolution of the nineteenth century in England, and that of the twentieth-century industrial revolutions in Russia and China, testify to the above. This analysis shows that the development patterns in the UDCs in recent times have not stimulated demand for labour, development process being essentially based on imported and sophisticated technology and capital which are products of a different historical and consequently of a different factor-endowment situation. N. Rosenberg in his work *Perspectives on Technology* observed: 'One must give up the notion that it is possible to analyse the effects of technological change independently of its context, since the same technology will have very different consequences in societies whose institutions, values, resource endowments and histories vary'.[45] We have explained why (i) the transfer of technology, capital and other resources has resulted in an almost instant growth of sophisticated industrial sectors in UDCs but has failed to stimulate effective demand for labour; (ii) the increasing pressure of population in these economies has failed to spur agricultural revolution leading to the industrial revolution. Because of negative impacts of technology and capital transfers, necessary reorganisation of the economy to generate indigenous technology to make more productive utilisation of domestic resources has failed to take place. Consequently, problems of so-called overpopulation and income inequality have been and are being aggravated and, therefore, the gap between rich and poor—intranational and international—is widening as days go by.

Appendix

Professor Hicks wrote: 'The whole industrial revolution of the last two hundred years has been nothing but a vast spectacular boom, largely induced by the unparalleled rise in population.'[46]

According to Habakkuk, the high rate of population growth certainly facilitated important developments in early industrialisation. In his view, early industrialisation produced higher levels of population.[47]

Habakkuk illustrated the above point:

One of the main sources of economic growth before the industrial revolution was the gradual extension of the market and the greater division of labour it promoted in the ways described long ago by Adam Smith. And the principal reason why this mechanism produced more rapid results in the period of the classic English Industrial Revolution was that a large number of canals were built. Canal building speeded up in the 1790s as opposed to, say, the 1750s not because of any technical improvements in their methods of construction or because it was easier to raise funds, but because the volume of traffic warranted it. And comparing the 1790s with the 1750s, one difference relevant to the volume of traffic was the greater density of population.[48]

Thomas McKeown and R.G. Ricon wrote:

Our knowledge of the birth rate and death rate in the first decades of the nineteenth century is in the same unsatisfactory state as in the eighteenth century. All that can be said with certainty is that the population was rising, and that the increase was attributable in large part to an excess of births over deaths established before 1800 and maintained thereafter.[49]

Notes

1. E. Boserup, *The Conditions of Agricultural Growth* (Chicago, 1965), p. 12.
2. H.J. Habakkuk, *Population Growth and Economic Development since 1750* (Leicester, 1971).
3. N. Tranter, *Population since the Industrial Revolution* (Croom Helm, London, 1973), p. 89. Tranter's survey of the period also mentions some other factors that stimulated population growth. These are: the age structure which had developed out of the 'bulge generation' created around the middle of the eighteenth century, and which was particularly suited to relatively high marriage and birth rates and low death rates; the lower mortality rate, achieved through the adoption of inoculation and vaccination against smallpox; the spread of the hospital movement, and the use of drugs like mercury, iron and chincone in medical treatment. All these features, however, indicate the general rise in the level of economic and social activity – a contribution of the agricultural and industrial revolution of the period which created tremendous demand for labour, particularly at a time when organisation, management and methods were simple, unsophisticated and labour-absorbing. See J.D. Chambers, *Population, Economy and Society in Pre-industrial England* (Oxford, 1972); T. McKeown and R.G. Brown, 'Medical Evidence related to English Population Change', *Population Studies*, IX (1955); P. Razzel, 'Population Change in Eighteenth Century England: A Reinterpretation', *Economic History Review*, XXVIII, no. 2 (1965).
4. Tranter, *Population*, p. 98.
5. Ibid., p. 79.

6. M. Drake, *Population and Society in Norway, 1735-1875* (Cambridge University Press, 1969).

7. Tranter, *Population*, p. 98.

8. Ibid., p. 79.

9. Habakkuk, *Growth and Development.*

10. J.D. Chambers, 'The Vale of Trent 1670-1800', *Economic History Review Supplement*, no. 3.

11. P. Bairoch, 'Agriculture and Industrial Revolution' in C.M. Cipolla (ed.), *The Industrial Revolution* (Fontana, London, 1973), pp. 488-92.

12. D.S. Landes, 'Industrialisation and Economic Development in Nineteenth Century Germany', *First International Conference on Economic History* (Stockholm, August 1960), pp. 85-6; P. Hohenberg, 'Changes in Rural France in the Period of Industrialisation, 1830-1940', *Journal of Economic History*, vol. 32 (1972), pp. 223-40; P. Maitra, 'Economic Development with or without an Industrial Revolution', *46th ANZAAS Congress Paper* (L'Bocconi University, Milan, 1977).

13. W.O. Henderson, *Britain and Industrial Europe, 1750-1870* (Liverpool University Press, 1954), pp. 139-67; A.H. Imlah, *Economic History Review*, IX (1952), p. 277. It has been noted by Henderson that in 1851 the extent to which manufacturers in Germany were content to imitate foreigners rather than stand on their own feet was commented on by Germans themselves. At the time of the Great Exhibition in London a German correspondent wrote to his paper: 'I cannot deny that German industry has no peculiar character. In the exhibition it appears as if every national characteristic were carefully avoided. Everywhere German industry appears to lean on some foreign industry and to imitate it. Here one beholds the supporting hand of France, there that of England'. (*Economist*, 28 June 1851.) Sir John Clapham commented on this, saying 'this is not a final verdict on the German industry of 1850-1 . . . but there is truth in it'. See J. Clapham, *The Wool and Worsted Industry* (1907).

14. Tranter, *Population*, pp. 146-53.

15. P. Maitra, 'Population, Poverty and Pollution', *Mainstream*, vol. 17 (1974), pp. 11-14.

16. H. Leibenstein, *The Impact of Population Growth on Economic Welfare in Rapid Population Growth Consequencies* (John Hopkins, Baltimore, 1971), pp. 188-9.

17. D. Thorner, 'The De-industrialisation of India', *First International Conference on Economic History* (Stockholm, August 1960), p. 70.

18. J.R. Hicks, *A Theory of Economic History* (Oxford, 1969), p. 165.

19. A.K. Bagchi, 'Industrialisation in India', *The Journal of Development Studies*, vol. 12, no. 2 (January 1976), pp. 132-50.

20. N.K. Sinha, *The Economic History of Bengal, 1793-1948* (Firma KLM, Calcutta, 1970), vol. 2.

21. Selections from the Records of Government, North Western Provinces, 1864, p. 116.

22. C. Clark, *The Conditions of Economic Progress* (Macmillan and Co., 1957), pp. 499 and 515.

23. C. Singer, 'East and West in Retrospect' in C. Singer *et al., A History of Technology* (Oxford, 1956), vol. 11.

24. Until the tenth century mills were used in the West for grinding grain. In contrast, the early information on water mills in China suggests that they were used not for turning simple millstones, but for more complicated functions such as blowing bellows in metalwork. The difference should not be surprising; the West in the dark ages was essentially agrarian and in comparison with China was poorer and underdeveloped. But as cities, trade and manufacturing grew in Europe from the tenth century onwards, motive power derived from hydraulic energy was

applied to an increasing variety of productive processes. See Singer *et al.*, *Technology*, pp. 160-1.

25. Ibid.

26. G.E. Walker, 'The Origins of the Machine Age', *History Today* (1966), pp. 591-2.

27. R. Benedict,*Race, Science and Politics* (The Viking Press, New York, 1959).

28. Boulding and Pfaff, p. 146.

29. B.H. Slicher van Bath, *The Agrarian History of Western Europe, AD 500-1850* (Arnold, 1963), pp. 239-41; I. Habib, *The Agrarian System of Moghul India, 1556-1707* (Asia Publishing, Bombay, 1963), p. 35.

30. H. Myint, *Economies of Developing Countries* (Hutchinson, London, 1964), pp. 29-30.

31. W.H. Moreland, *India at the Time of Akbar* (H. Ram, Delhi, 1962); P. Jehangir, *India* (Cambridge, 1925), pp. 60-1.

32. K. Marx, *Capital*, 1st edn (1867), vol. 1, pp. 563-4.

33. E.L. Jones and S.J. Woolf (eds.), *The Historical Role of Agrarian Change in Economic Development* (Methuen, London, 1969), p. 1.

34. L. Cottrell, *The Tiger of China* (London, 1964), p. 131.

35. Jones and Woolf, *Agrarian Change*, p. 2.

36. Ibid., p. 2.

37. Ibid., p. 2.

38. Until 1740, the population of Europe increased very slowly, as it had in the previous century, death rate cancelling out birth rate, which characterises a low-level equilibrium situation. However, from about 1750 onwards, when Europe had some 120-140 million inhabitants, the rate of growth began to accelerate rapidly so that, by 1800, the population had increased to about 190 million. In other words, the growth rate must have doubled within 50 years. It is to be noted here that Malthus wrote his doomsday thesis on population in 1798. See Cipolla, *Industrial Revolution*, pp. 27-9.

39. P. Bairoch, 'Agriculture and the Industrial Revolution 1700-1914' in Cipolla; E.J. Hobsbawm, *The Age of Revolution* (Weidenfeld, 1962), p. 31.

40. Cipolla, *Industrial Revolution*, pp. 27-8.

41. Maitra, 'Poverty and Pollution', pp. 11-14.

42. C. Futardo, *Economic Development in Latin America* (Cambridge University Press, 1970), pp. 27-34.

43. P. Bairoch, *The Economic Development of the Third World* (Methuen, London, 1973), pp. 50-1.

44. This is, however, not applicable to newly settled countries where modern sectors were imported lock, stock and barrel (i.e. capital, technology and human resources) and as a result local economies have remained depressed since then. For example, the Indians in the USA and Canada, the Eskimo economy, and the Aborigines and Maoris in Australasia. However, the modern sector in these countries has maintained its Anglicised culture and ways of life and the indigenous people are facing the problem of identity.

45. N. Rosenberg, *Perspectives on Technology* (Cambridge University Press, 1976), p. 2.

46. Hicks, *A Theory of Economic History*, p. 285.

47. H.J. Habakkuk, 'Population Problems and Economic Development' in S. Liberman (ed.), *Europe and the Industrial Revolution* (Schenkman Publishing Company, Cambridge, 1972), p. 285.

48. Ibid., p. 286.

49. T. McKeown and R.G. Ricon, *The Decline of Mortality in England and Wales*, p. 311.

4 WESTERN CAPITAL, UNDERDEVELOPMENT, MARX AND MARXISTS

In this chapter we will deal with the underdevelopment of India in terms of Marx's prediction that 'the bourgeoisie by the rapid development of all instruments of production, by the immensely facilitated means of communication draws all, even the most barbarian nations, into civilization . . . the railway system will therefore, become, in India, truly the forerunner of modern industry'.[1] But western capitalism failed to produce a cumulative cycle of investment leading to the regeneration of India's economy (or of all erstwhile colonies, for that matter) that was stagnating under feudalism, as predicted by Marx. Later Marxists, however, have tried to explain the causes of the failure in different terms, i.e. (i) removal and expropriation of affected countries' previously accumulated surplus, and underdevelopment as the result of development;[2] (ii) unequal exchange between developed and underdeveloped countries and thus, the improved living standards of the working class of the developed countries are paid for by the underdeveloped countries;[3] (iii) not by simple exploitation but by insufficient exploitation.[4] In this chapter I shall try to explain the views of these Marxists in the light of my discussion in Chapter 3.

The problem of underdevelopment was scarcely dealt with in classical Marxist writings of the nineteenth century. This is not unexpected, as the phenomena of development and underdevelopment, in the sense they are understood today, were hardly distinguishable at that time. There were, however, two different worlds in existence at that time; both were at the pre-industrial stage. There were colonies and colonial powers; both had feudalism as the basis of socio-economic and political organisations, and the power of mercantile capitalism was on the rise in both sets of countries. In this circumstance, it is not expected that there will be any impact of the rule of feudal colonial powers in colonies in terms of bringing about any fundamental changes in the existing production techniques leading to changes in socio-economic political order in the colonies. Rather, the feudal colonial power left the colonies undisturbed socially, politically and economically, unlike the changes that took place when the countries of industrial capitalism became the colonial powers after the nineteenth century. The latter introduced a new method of production, i.e. industrialisation which, however, remained confined to a small part of the total economy and thus failed to produce the force of regeneration as Marx predicted. However, in some colonies in the pre-industrial period, Portuguese and Spanish colonial powers in Latin America, for example, there was a serious impact in terms of depopulation that affected the future development of these areas. C. Furtado wrote:

> It is now generally accepted that the population of Spanish America at the time of independence (later 19th century) was much smaller than when America was discovered. The particular circumstance of the Spanish conquest and of the subsequent occupation of the more densely populated areas produced what amounts to a virtual holocaust of the indigenous population. The native populations at the time of the conquest were concentrated in mountainous regions, supported by artisan agricultural economies, using elaborate techniques for the utilization of soil and water and characterised by complex systems of social organization. The mining economy introduced by the Span-iards, which required a widescale dislocation of the population, dis-rupted the pattern of food production and led to the break-up of the family units among a sizeable proportion of the population. The actual process of conquest resulted in the forcible transfer of great numbers of people, particularly adult males, who were practically wiped out by the long marches and forced labour imposed upon them by the conquistadores. On the other hand, the need to extract a surplus from the population remaining on the land, in order to pro-vide a steady food supply for the mining community and city, made heavy demands on the remaining rural population. Finally, the ravages of epidemics caused by contact with people carrying new contagious diseases played a no less significant part in bringing about a holocaust of the Indian population. It has been estimated, for example, that the Mexican population, which was probably not less than some 16 million at the time of conquest was reduced to one-tenth of this total in the course of a century.[5]

However, as history shows, under the impact of the spread of Western capitalism, the indigenous process of development in colonies and other affected countries has been stunted since the late nineteenth century. Economic history of most of the Third World countries before they were introduced to Western capitalism shows that they had elaborate agricultural techniques; efficient proto-industries and complex social organisations. Population pressure at that time, however, was not enough to spur the prevailing agricultural organisation and techniques to the industrial revolution as it did in the UK. In the case of Latin American and African countries (the population growth of the latter countries was seriously impaired by the slave trade), however, population rather declined for reasons stated before which thereby affected the course of their natural development. Hobsbawm wrote about the level of technology, methods of production etc. at the time of the industrial revolution as mentioned earlier in this book.

Marx grew up during the process of the Industrial Revolution in England and the Marxist theory as presented in the *Communist Manifesto* dealt directly but briefly with the spread of capitalism throughout the world and appeared to anticipate not underdevelopment but development. Marx and Engels wrote in the *Communist Manifesto* in 1848:

The bourgeoisie, by the rapid development of all instruments of production, by the immensely facilitated means of communication, drew all, even the most barbarous nations into civilization . . . It compels all nations, on pain of extinction, to adopt the bourgeois mode of production; it compels them to introduce what it calls civilization into their midst—i.e. they become bourgeois themselves. In one word, it creates a world after its own image.[6]

Latterly, in more concrete terms, Marx elaborated this view in an article on 'Future Results of British Rule in India'.

I know that the English aristocracy intend to endow India with railways with the exclusive view of extracting at diminishing expense the cotton and other raw materials for their manufacture. But when you have once introduced machinery into the locomotion of a country, which possesses iron and coals, you are unable to withhold it from its fabrication. You cannot maintain a net of railways over an immense country without introducing all those industrial processes necessary to meet the immediate and current wants of railway locomotion and out of which there must grow the application of machinery to those branches of industry not immediately connected with railways. The railway system will, therefore, become, in India, truly the forerunner of modern industry.[7]

And later in 1867 in the preface to *Capital* Marx wrote:

The country that is more developed industrially only shows to the less developed, the image of its own future.[8]

Thus, it appears that Marx thought that the spread of the 'reproductive power', i.e. industrialisation, was inevitable in India as a result of investment by British capitalists. There is no doubt about the fact that there had been some growth of modern industries during this period, mainly confined to light consumer goods production, railways and communication, cash crop production, but in the process it had absorbed a negligible proportion of the labour force into manufacturing, contributing less than 2 to 3 per cent. This proportion of the non-agricultural labour force was much larger, being about 26 to 30 per cent before the introduction of modern industries (discussed in connection with the phenomenon of industrialisation in India in Chapter 3).

However, Marx qualified his above observations, pointing out that the process would not benefit the masses directly, as all the English bourgeoisie may be forced to do will neither emancipate nor materially mend the social condition of the mass of the people, depending not only on the development of the 'reproductive powers', but on their appreciation by the people. But what it will not fail to do is to lay down the premisses for both. As we have noted, however, the premisses laid down were not historically rooted to the past of the countries concerned and therefore they failed to spur on these countries to dynamic industrial development.

It is well known today that the process not only did not benefit the masses, but also had an indirect effect of retarding the growth of indigenous forces of regeneration and industrialisation. The process of industrialisation that was introduced into France or Germany, for example, from the UK in the nineteenth century, however, had the effect of fully-fledged industrial development. It took place through trade and not under colonial relationships. (Discussed in Chapter 3.) Population pressure in these economies led to changes in agrarian organisation and production relations and, thereby, prepared them for industrial development. Secondly, the industrial capital and skill introduced from the UK was simple and labour-absorbing and thus it helped in utilising the human resources released from the shackles of feudalism for laying down the foundations for industrial development.

It is to be noted here, too, that capitalism was at its nascent stage and the production process was largely based on more productive utilisation of labour resources. But in the subsequent period of capitalism (i.e. monopoly capitalism) labour-dispensing capital-intensive technology evolved to meet growing international markets for manufacturing goods, production of which was kept confined to a handful of countries. But Marx made it clear that industrialisation in India (development of the reproductive powers) would only come about at a 'more or less remote period', when he said, 'We may safely expect to see . . . the regeneration of that great and interesting country [i.e. India] as a result.' History shows that the regeneration has not come about in these countries even today, when 80 per cent of the total population are still dependent on stagnant, under-developed agricultural sectors for a living. Although it is true that a very limited but highly sophisticated modern sector has been created as a consequence of the introduction of Western industrial capitalism, obviously it had neither the objective nor the effect of utilising human resources.

Lenin also had a point to make in this connection. When capitalism reached the stage of imperialism because of its inner contradiction resulting from its inevitable urge for survival and expansion, Lenin wrote that the export of capital influences greatly accelerates the development of capitalism in those countries to which it is exported. While, therefore, the export of capital may tend, to a certain extent, to arrest development in the capital-exporting countries, it can only do so by expanding and deepening the further development of capitalism throughout the world.[9] There is no doubt about the fact that capitalism grew in these countries but it is equally true that it has been confined to a very negligible proportion of the total population and of the economy.

Marxists are aware today that by exporting capital and technology in its mature stage Western capitalism has been able to export miseries and unemployment from their own countries to importing underdeveloped countries and thus, it has been able to lessen the state of increasing immiseration in its economics as predicted by Marx. It is also not borne out by the evidence, as claimed by Lenin, that the export of capital tends to a certain degree to arrest development in capital-exporting countries.[10] Rather the picture is just the opposite for economic reasons. The export of capital, technology and other goods is largely responsible for full employment and the prosperity under monopoly capitalism in the West and for the widening gap between developed and underdeveloped nations. This is the inevitable result of the deliberate policy of Western capitalism. Rapidly increasing capital-intensity of production needs ever expanding markets. Capitalist countries by exporting capital have made importing underdeveloped countries perpetually dependent on them first for capital and then for technology, as well as markets for their finished products. Developed capitalist countries constitute today only about 20 per cent of all nations of the world and supply more than 90 per cent of world manufactures. And so long as this dependence continues to dominate the relationship with the Third World countries, capitalism in the industrialised countries will never face any serious threat to its survival and expansion.

According to Paul Baran, the most influential Marxist interpreter of underdevelopment, India (and all underdeveloped countries for that matter) has been prevented from developing and regenerating as a result of the introduction of such industrialisation. India experienced only the destruction of her traditional economy and society and after that nothing but 'the chronic catastrophe of the last two centuries'. The reason for this, as advanced by Paul Baran, differs from what Marx thought. According to Baran, a large share of accumulated capital, i.e. the capital accumulated in India, was not reinvested there. He wrote:

> There can be no doubt that had the amount of economic surplus that Britain has torn from India been invested in India, India's economic development to date would have borne little similarity to the actual sombre record.[11]

Paul Baran's view in connection with the failure of Western capitalists' presence in Asia, Africa and Latin America to create a cumulative process of capitalist development there, was that either they found 'established societies with rich and ancient cultures', or 'the general conditions and in particular the climate were such as to preclude any mass settlement of Western European arrivals . . . consequently, the Western European visitors rapidly determined to extract the largest possible gains from the host countries, and to take the loot home'.[12] This is Baran's view of the first phase of capitalist exploitation of Asia, Africa, and Latin American countries. Most Marxists are in complete agreement with his exploitation theory. Western capitalism reached the stage of monopoly capitalism in the early twentieth century which is most evident in the form of labour-dispensing sophisticated technology.

Concerning the impact of Western capitalism on colonies when it reached the next stage of monopoly capitalism and imperialism, Baran wrote that

> the rule of monopoly capitalism and imperialism in the advanced countries and economic and social backwardness in the underdeveloped countries are immediately related, representing merely different aspects of what is in reality a global problem.[13]

Baran's analysis is thus seriously limited by the absence of two very important factors: (i) he did not consider the level of technology introduced in India and its effectiveness in utilising more productively its domestic resources. Regeneration of India could have taken place as Marx predicted provided the industrial investment resulted in more productive use of the human resources of India, thereby laying down the premiss for regeneration: (ii) no consideration has been given to the question of the source of investment in Baran's analysis. When the source of capital investment is foreign and not domestic (i.e. it is not a result of more productive utilisation of domestic labour resources), then the capital investment cannot have the desired effect of regeneration of the country. It simply leads to the building up of an island of modern capitalism which is not rooted in the history of the economy and it acts as the greatest hindrance to the growth of the indigenous reproductive power and thereby to the regeneration of the country. This is evident today in all Third World countries whether they receive aid from the capitalist West or from socialist blocks and whether the surplus generated in this process of investment is withdrawn or reinvested. Baran's main thesis, is, therefore, that the removal of a large share of the affected countries' previously accumulated and generated surplus is largely responsible for the failure of Western capitalism to cause a cumulative cycle of investment leading to the regeneration of these economies stagnating under feudalism.

However, Baran accepts the fact that capitalism forced the diversion of some of this economic surplus to the improvement of their system of communications, to the building of railways, harbours, and highways, providing thereby, as a by-product, the facilities needed for profitable production and 'a powerful impetus to the development of capitalism'. But, according to Baran, 'this development was forcibly shunted off its normal course, distorted and crippled to suit the purpose of Western imperialism'. In other words, Baran thinks that had there been no removal of surplus from these countries and instead, had there been reinvestment of these surpluses, these economies could have been transformed into reproductive (i.e. industrialised) ones as Marx predicted. There is no doubt about the fact that there had been tremendous exploitation and removal of loot from these countries, which surely was responsible for their increasing impoverishment. But the question remains— could industrialism or capitalism, a product of external economic forces and history imposed from outside, lead to regeneration, even if surplus produced in the process is reinvested? Another intriguing question involving the earnings from exports of products of Western investment in these countries is whether investment of these export earnings in the form of imports of consumer goods or even capital goods could lead to development. Apparently it has not done so. I will discuss this question later. I must now present views of other prominent Marxists particularly of Frank, Kay and Emmanuel.

Frank has taken a stand in this respect which is more or less identical to that of Baran's. He interpreted the process as follows: the metropolis (developed economies) expropriates economic surplus from its satellites (i.e. underdeveloped economies) and appropriates it for its own economic development. The satellites remain underdeveloped for lack of access to their own surplus and as a consequence of the same polarisation and exploitative contradiction which the metropolis introduces and maintains in the satellite's domestic structure. The combination of these contradictions, once firmly implanted, reinforces the processes of development in the increasingly dominant metropolis and underdevelopment in the even more dependent satellites until they are resolved through the abandonment of capitalism by one or both interdependent parts. This is one side, though a very important side, of the picture, which, however, is seriously limited by the absence of the exposition of the most basic aspect of this process of polarisation between rich and poor nations. Frank's analysis does not tell anything about the effects of technology. (See Chapter 3.)

Supporting the view that exploitation of colonies by Western capitalism is the basic factor responsible for the failure of industrialisation introduced by the West in colonies to produce the effects of a cumulative cycle of investment leading to the regeneration of these countries as predicted by Marx, Emmanuel focuses on trade as a mechanism of exploitation of underdeveloped countries by developed countries. Emmanuel's thesis is that the underdeveloped countries are exploited through unequal exchange. The developed countries sell commodities to the underdeveloped countries at prices that exceed their values and buy from them commodities at prices below values, so that every transaction, between the two sets of countries, involves a drain of value out of the underdeveloped countries and thus reduces the pace of accumulation there. This is Emmanuel's unequal-exchange thesis in the narrow sense. In the broad sense of the term, Emmanuel claims that the improved living standards of the working class in the developed countries are paid for, in part at least, by the underdeveloped countries. Emmanuel's thesis that the working class in the industrialised countries has benefited from such exploitation in terms of a higher level of living and full employment conditions, agrees with Marx's contention of the increasing miseries of the working class when it is considered globally. Because of the transfer of capital and technology resulting from the rapid growth of trade and foreign investment etc., the life blood of capitalism in its mature stage, fuller employment of resources and a higher level of living for the working class in the developed countries have been possible but at the cost of increasing impoverishment and underemployment of the labour force in underdeveloped countries. But this is one side of the picture. The other and more important side of the unequal-exchange thesis, is that even if the exchange between developed and underdeveloped countries were equal, would this equality in exchange have led to the development of underdeveloped countries? We have discussed this aspect elsewhere.

Kay's position is somewhat different. According to him, development of colonies has been thwarted because capitalist exploitation was not sufficient. He elaborates his point thus: underdevelopment is explained as the result of capital expanding from its home lands in the form of merchant capital which drew surplus value out of the under-developed countries without being able to revolutionise the mode of production. Furthermore, when an attempt was made at such a revolution in the period after the last war through a strategy of industrialisation, it could only reinforce the conditions of underdevelopment that already existed.

We have noticed that there are two sets of argument: one regards exploitation and removal of surplus produced by Western investment as being responsible for underdevelopment and rapid development of the West; the other is the argument of unequal exchange — resulting from the exploitation of the working class of underdeveloped countries.

If we explain why Marx's prediction did not materialise, it will help in explaining the limitations of Baran, Frank, Emmanuel and Kay.

It is well known today that the introduction of modern industry, particularly railways, into the colonies did not unleash forces of regeneration and a cumulative cycle of investment in underdeveloped countries. However, such introduction in the mid-nineteenth century in Western Europe, for example, Germany and France, revolutionised modes of production leading to development. The reasons are discussed in the previous chapter.

There is no doubt about the fact that the exploitation and looting of precious metals and other resources from these countries at the mercantile stage has impoverished their economies, and thus deprived them of vast resources that could have been used to transform them into reproductive countries when the need arose with the increasing pressure of population on existing resources. In this way, technology and more productive machines could have evolved indigenously and produced the regenerative effects.

The modern industries and railways which were introduced into India by the 'English millocracy' were products of investment of surplus resulting from the increased productivity generated by the Industrial Revolution in the UK. Needless to say that these were not the results of increased productivity of India's indigenous resources, and therefore, the capitalist investment from outside had failed to generate a cumulative cycle of investment in India. It had created only an island of so-called 'modern sector' completely dislinked with the local economy. Investment in the production of cash crops thus had very little relation with the evolution of the local economy and did not cause the transformation of India into a reproductive country initially.

This is the first stage of English investment in India (exports of these goods not being a product of the use of indigenous resources) and the capital from abroad had little effect in terms of transforming India into a reproductive country.

The second stage is marked by the investment of capital goods to produce consumer goods. Marx wrote:

> When you have introduced machinery into the locomotion of a country, which possesses iron and coals, you are unable to withhold it from its fabrication.

In fact, Marx was quite right, as history shows that modern manufacturing industries began to grow, though slowly, in the latter part of the nineteenth century but rapidly since the 1950s. But this had not led to the regeneration and transformation of India into a reproductive country, because of the reasons stated before. One important point to be noted here is that these investment resources and productivity were not generated indigenously, and hence had no linkage effects. Even if profits that were earned through exports were reinvested (in fact, according to recent studies, a large portion was reinvested) it would not have led to what Marx or Baran expected to have happened. The reason is that the imports of consumer goods and capital goods earned as export earnings and their use within India's economy could not have diffusion effects resulting in cumulative investment effects, because non-indigenous sources of origin of capital and technology were used.

There is no doubt about the fact that British capital (e.g. the railways) introduced in the Western European countries in the mid-nineteenth century became the forerunner of modern industry in Europe. But European countries earned capital, machineries, railways, etc., through exports of their domestic products produced by their own inputs and thus raised the level of income of all factors of production. This helped them to absorb the foreign capital and technology which was labour using and not labour dispensing as it is today, and avoided the perpetuation of an island of the imported modern sector surrounded by a vast and expanding sea of the underdeveloped traditional sector.

These schools of Marxists did not take into consideration the fundamental aspect related to the question of the sources of investment (i.e. whether it is generated indigenously or externally) and the level of technology. If the industrial investment was the result of surpluses produced within the economy by natural and human resources through their interaction, as happened in the UK and in other European countries, investment of that surplus would have created the desired effect. Industrial investment of the period under reference in India and other underdeveloped countries, in so-called 'modern' activities such as crop plantation, railways and communications, etc., was undertaken not to meet the needs of the local economy, neither was it a result of increased productivity of domestic resources. The surplus that was invested in these economies was generated elsewhere. Capitalism in the nineteenth century could produce the effects of regeneration as envisaged by Marx if it had resulted from the evolution of the domestic economy.

Then we should also take note of the effects of changes in technology. This is very important in the sense that when Western capitalism reached the stage of monopoly capitalism and imperialism as depicted by Baran and Frank, capital and technology became increasingly labour dispensing.[14] When these types of capital and technology were supplied to the underdeveloped countries by the Western industrialised countries they had very limited effects in terms of absorbing labour resources of former countries and thus failed to produce any effects of their regeneration.

We have now discussed recent works by different schools of Marxists on this aspect, and see that they have given us a partial picture of the phenomena of underdevelopment and its perpetuation. Discussion in the previous chapters will help us in understanding the basic nature of the problem of development and another important aspect related to the above, i.e. impacts of capital investment by a socialist country (e.g. USSR) in a socialist country (e.g. China in the 1950s and early 1960s) and in a non-socialist country (e.g. India).

Notes

1. K. Marx and F. Engels, *The Communist Manifesto, 1848* (Penguin, Harmondsworth, 1973), p. 71; K. Marx, *Surveys from Exile* (Penguin, Harmondsworth, 1973), p. 341.

2. P. Baran, *The Political Economy of Growth* (Monthly Review Press, New York, 1962); A.G. Frank, *Capitalism and Underdevelopment in Latin America* (Pelican, London, 1969).

3. A. Emmanuel, *Unequal Exchange* (London, 1972).

4. G. Kay, *Development and Underdevelopment* (Macmillan, London, 1975).

5. C. Futardo, *The Economic Development of Latin America* (Cambridge University Press, 1970), p. 6.

6. Marx and Engels, *Communist Manifesto*, p. 71.

7. Marx, *Exile*, pp. 323-41.

8. K. Marx, *Capital*, 1st edn (1867), vol. 1, p. xvii.

9. V.I. Lenin, *Imperialism, The Highest Stage of Capitalism* (London, 1934), p. 107.

10. 'While the export of capital is able to a certain extent to arrest development in the exporting countries, this can, however, take place only at the cost of a broadening and deepening of the further development of capitalism throughout the world.' Ibid., p. 59.

11. Baran, *Economy of Growth*, p. 48.

12. Ibid., p. 42.

13. Ibid., p. 44.

14. 'In proportion as capital accumulates, the lot of the labourer, be his payment high or low, must grow worse.' Marx, *Capital*, vol. 1, p. 661. This aspect may be understood better with the help of this Marxist interpretation of the phenomenon. The more productive forces are developed, the more the proletariat is exploited, that is, the higher the proportion of surplus labour to necessary labour. See C. Bethleheim, *The Transition from Capitalism to Socialism* (Monthly Review Press, New York, 1971).

5 INDUSTRIAL REVOLUTION IN THE TWENTIETH CENTURY: SOVIET RUSSIA

Russia prior to 1917 was basically a country similar to India with a small per capita national income and a low standard of living due to its low level of productivity. Income per head was about 102 roubles or scarcely more than a third of that of Germany, less than a quarter that of England and about a seventh of that of the USA at that date.[1] Because of the economic organisation, the condition of the general masses of the population was appallingly poor. Industry was little developed, based as it was on foreign capital, and the overwhelming majority of the population were engaged on the land. Obviously agriculture had a very low yield in relation both to manpower and to acreage. This suggests that there was an excess population relative to both the cultivated area available and to the means of production in the hands of the cultivators. Heavy industry, weakly developed, was geared to the needs of railway construction which again was undertaken essentially to serve the interests of the export/import trade and the landed aristocracy. Agriculture was largely dominated by the export market; the country remained overwhelmingly dependent upon the imports for the supply of a wide range of consumer goods and some capital goods but these had very little to do with the large masses of population involved in agricultural production.[2]

It is characteristic of such countries (which were under the spell of imported industrialisation and as a consequence could not generate indigenous forces leading to industrial revolution) that they tended to suffer from rural overpopulation or a surplus labour force consisting of persons who were either landless and gained such livelihood as they could by intermittent employment (mainly seasonal) or were cultivators of small plots of land using primitive methods and inadequate equipment. In either case the productivity of labour was exceedingly low and their shift to industrial construction would cause a negligible fall in output. Rather it would help to reorganise the plots of land with a view to utilising the labour left more productively. Dobb wrote: 'Given a measure of re-organisation in the social and property relations of the village – an extension of agricultural co-operation and some consolidation of parcellated and scattered holdings, permitting a more rational utilisation of labour – the transfer of labour from village to town can march in company with an actual increase in the output of agriculture.'[3] In other words, the problem of so-called overpopulation can only be solved by making labour more productive, which necessitates fundamental changes in economic organisation to produce resources for industrial and agricultural development. This requires the development of indigenous technology suitable to the reorganised economic structure and changed factor endowment. The extremely low average standard of living in Tsarist Russia may be explained by the low productivity of her agriculture which was the source of livelihood for 80 per cent of her population. For an agricultural country, particularly a grain-exporting country, Russia's population density was relatively great; that of European Russia (excluding Poland) at the end of the nineteenth century being 53.5 per square mile against 31 in the USA. Moreover, the proportion of the total land that was cultivated was also relatively small, being no more than 25 per cent even in European Russia, compared with nearly 40 per cent in France and Germany. Consequently, the average area of cultivated land per head of the agricultural population worked out at a figure of only about three acres compared with about 13 acres in the USA, eight acres in Denmark and four acres in France and Germany. According to another estimate, in the Ukraine the area of cultivated land per head of the agricultural population was as small as 1½ acres.[4] At the same time the average yield per acre of arable land in European Russia was no more than about eight to ten bushels, which was hardly more than a quarter of the yield per acre in the UK, a third of that of Eastern Germany and half that of France. Prianishnikov and Lebediantsev concluded that Russia's agriculture 'combined the negative features of European agriculture (relative smallness of arable area) and of American agriculture (lowness of yield) with a resulting level of grain production per head appropriate to a country importing grain, instead of exporting it'.[5]

The chronic deficiency and low level of capital among all peasants except a thin upper layer also accounted for the low productivity. Half of the peasants used a primitive type of wooden plough (called the *sokha*) and the sowing was by hand. The major part of the harvesting and even of the threshing was laboriously done by hand with a sickle and the centuries-old hand flail. There was on average one reaper to every 26 peasant farms, one threshing machine to every 29 and one mower to every 100. In this respect the larger estates and the well-to-do Kulaks' farms were better situated and the yield per acre on them was generally somewhat higher than the average.[6] What we saw in underdeveloped countries in the 1950s is just an enlarged photo-copy of the conditions of agriculture in pre-1917 Russia.

The Kulaks, or rich peasants, were responsible for most of the marketed produce and the poorer peasantry, who constituted the vast majority
of the agricultural population, were primarily subsistence farmers. Two
thirds of the total agricultural produce came from peasant land and one
third from the large estates but this produce was marketed in reverse
proportion. This reflects an acute inequality in land ownership, income
and yield and the tendency on the part of the large estates to under-
take the cultivation of specialised crops for export markets to import
consumer goods.

According to an inquiry report of the Central Statistical Committee
relating to 1905 concerning 50 provinces, the richer ten per cent of
peasant households, each possessing about 55 acres of cultivated land,
owned some 35 per cent of all land, while the smallest holders of all,
possessing less than ten acres, constituted one sixth of the peasantry
but owned even less than four per cent of the land. Fifty per cent of
peasant households had plots of land of about 22 acres which occupied
just over a fifth of the total area.[7]

In Russia, modern industries were introduced during the late nineteenth century. These were largely based on foreign capital. Foreign
capital played a very significant role in Russian industry before the
Revolution. One third of the total capital invested in the industrial
sector in Russia was held by foreigners in 1914.[8] The proportion was
much larger in the nineteenth century. These industries served the consumer interests of the landed aristocracy, merchant class and other
upper-income groups. The internal market was not large enough because
of the limited employment effects of this type of industrialisation, and
consequently people depending on agriculture began to create a growing
pressure on agriculture.[9]

The industrialisation pattern in pre-Revolution days in Russia was
the same as was the case with other industrial latecomers of the nineteenth century, except for the fact that other countries became successful industrialisers and Russia failed. Modern industrial production had
been advancing rapidly, since the 1880s in particular. But the agricultural
sector showed little progress. Dobb wrote that wheat yields per acre
were no higher than those of India. The average yield of arable land was
only a third of Germany and half that of France. Farming techniques
were primitive and most peasants used wooden ploughs, owned only
one or no draught animals and cultivated inefficient strip fields on
scattered holdings. Yet Russia was the world's largest grain exporter in
the decade before 1914.

The modern industry in certain regions of Russia had shown a quite

remarkable development, particularly since the 1880s; in the coal and
iron region of the Donetz and Dnieper in the south, in the Moscow region
and the neighbourhood of St Petersburg and in Poland. 'Much of this
modern industry was characterised by a high level of concentration both
of production and of ownership and control.'[10]

Firms were large; for example the proportion of all workers in
factories who were employed in enterprises with more than 500 workers reached the surprisingly high figure of 53 per cent.[11] By the end of
the nineteenth century, there had been a good deal of railway construction, which in mileage reached an impressive total. By 1903 there were
some 40,000 miles of railway in existence (about two thirds state operated in the area of the Russian Empire), which by 1914 had been increased by a further 8,000-odd miles.[12]

In contrast, road development was strikingly primitive. There were
less than 20,000 miles of regular roads and of these scarcely more than
3,000 were surfaced in the West European manner. In cases of imported
industrialisation this must be the pattern. If we look at the underdeveloped countries of today we notice substantial development in railways
and air traffic (with airports in most commercial centres) on the one
hand, and poor road development that serves more than 75 per cent of
the economy on the other. As regards roads, Russia was for the most
part still in the position of England in the mid-eighteenth century.
Obviously the iron and steel industries in Russia owed their origin to
the needs of railway construction. Needless to say, industrialisation in
Russia had touched little more than the surface of Russia's economic
system; this would, however, be expected of such imported industrialisation. The obvious consequence of such development was the growth
of patches of factory industry which were no more than industrial
islands surrounded by a vast agricultural sea. Less than 15 per cent of
the population lived in towns, and less than ten per cent of its total
labour force were industrial workers. And of these industrial workers,
a large number were of a migratory nature, in the sense that they still
had economic links with the village and often returned there in the
summer to help their families with the harvest. Dobb quotes an investigation report of 1910 which states that as many as two thirds of the
factory workers of St Petersburg retained nominal ownership of some
village land, and nearly a fifth of them returned to the village every
summer.[13] The same description is equally applicable to industrial
workers in underdeveloped countries today. This also indicates the
nature of the industries, which were mostly foreign importations:
foreign owned, foreign financed and staffed by foreign managerial and

technical personnel and primarily intended for foreign markets. Side by side with these giant factories, there were household handicraft industries as well as small-scale factories with no more than sixteen employees. Nearly 20 per cent of the labour force was employed in these non-factory and small factory establishments, though often part time.

In 1913 nine iron and steel plants accounted for more than half the production of pig iron. Nearly 90 per cent of the production of rails came from seven firms. Taking Russian factory industry as a whole (exclusive of mining), the horse power per worker was about three-fifths of the equivalent figure in England and only a third of that in American industry.[14]

As pointed out earlier, foreign capital dominated the industrial sectors. Major foreign firms came from the West European business elite in the pursuit of the entrepreneurial profits which were believed to be associated with advanced industrial techniques. These were implemented by foreign skills on all levels. It has been claimed that the continuing historical contact of industrially advanced nations with underdeveloped ones has hastened technical modernisation – the key to economic progress. It is true that this contact has led to the growth of islands of modernisation but these have miserably failed to spread in the economy. W. Parker raised a relevant question: 'The question which might be intriguing is why, given this transfer of techniques, was not progress even faster and the spread of new methods among native Russian firms more extensive?'[15] This same question is troubling modern underdeveloped countries more today than it did in the late nineteenth century. H.J. Ellison wrote in this connection:

> The conception of economic modernisation employed incorporates a broad range of economic changes – agricultural, industrial, trade and financial, which began in Western Europe in the late middle ages and reached a new stage in the nineteenth century with the fruition of the agricultural and industrial revolution. An impressive Russian modernisation (though not a unique one, since it applies to most countries which followed the European states into the sphere of modern economic life) is the incredible mixture and the kaleidoscopic quality of the changing economic scene. Thus modern industry began with serf labour and serfdom survived into the period of modern industrial infrastructure. Or, take another example, large scale factory manufacturing appeared before there was any development of cottage industry.[16]

In 1860 the mining industry continued to rely heavily upon serf labour, about 70 per cent of its workers being serfs, while only 27 per cent of manufacturing labourers were serfs. The most spectacular industrial advance of the first half of the nineteenth century was the growth of the textile industry, particularly of cotton; by 1860 two thirds of manufacturing workers were employed in textiles. The factories were generally rather large, with as many as 1,000 workers, and employed mainly serf labour.

The country remained predominantly agricultural, with not more than nine million (or less than eight per cent) of its inhabitants directly or indirectly involved in the operation of the industrial system.[17]

By 1914 there were 327 foreign joint-stock companies with an aggregate capital of 1,343 billion roubles, and one third of the capital of Russian industry was foreign.[18]

Sergei Witte, Minister of Finance from 1892 to 1903, saw Russia occupying the economic status of a colony, supplying the developed states of Europe with raw materials while herself importing manufactured goods.[19]

The Russian industrial revolution since the 1920s was attempted in a socialist framework and as such it might appear paradoxical to any orthodox Marxist that when a country was preparing for a socialist revolution, peasant agriculture was still dominant. It is not difficult to explain the paradox today. Industrialisation and peasant farming had co-existed since the introduction of industries to Russia in the late nineteenth century. Industrialisation, being imported, had not evolved out of the development of agriculture and nor did it help agricultural development.

Industrial growth based on imported capital and technology accelerated, but it remained confined to a very limited area because of the lack of diffusion of such industrialisation, and so agriculture could not progress from peasant farming due to the increasing pressure of population and the lack of non-agricultural employment opportunities. The increasing population could not be absorbed in this process of industrialisation. This may be shown by the sectoral distribution of the labour force. In terms of the proportion of the labour in agriculture, the Russian economy on the eve of the plan for industrial revolution (i.e. 1928) was far less industrialised than were other major economies at comparable levels of per capita income. This problem is more acute today, since the 1950s, than it was in the pre-World War II period. This is due to the differences in technology of the two periods, implying that in the past the technology, though imported, was relatively labour-absorbing.

This paradoxical development raised a long controversy over the process of industrialisation in Soviet Russia on the eve of launching the first

Five Year Plan. In the first place, the possibilities of developing heavy industries by importing capital goods from abroad was severely restricted by reason of the reluctance to grant loans to the USSR on the part of the industrial world. This attitude also hindered the possibility of financing import surplus by foreign borrowing. Therefore Soviet Russia had to find the resources for industrial development almost exclusively from internal sources.

Consequently surplus human resources in peasant farming were considered to be an economic asset, which was mobilised through the introduction of vigorous and fundamental changes in agrarian organisation in the form of collectives. This approach is considered as the pre-condition for industrial revolution in the twentieth century. Collectivisation not only helped mobilisation of surplus labour for industrial construction work but also made possible the more productive utilisation of resources left in farming. Dobb wrote: 'To a large extent this [the collectives] was an economic asset, since it facilitated the centralised planning of construction without which the impressive development of the years from 1928 to 1941 would scarcely have been conceivable.'[20] It was recognised that all the agricultural surplus required for industrial development could not be mobilised by encouraging the growth of large-scale individual farming which would have distorted the supply of surplus to industry and the towns and thereby made it difficult to mobilise resources for more productive use. Dobb wrote that 'for this reason it proved necessary for the Soviet economy simultaneously to carry through a policy of high speed industrialisation and a socio-economic revolution in peasant farming to release resources for industrial growth'.[21] The argument rests on the fact that the economic system contains elements of reserve productive capacity (unutilised or underutilised labour and resources) which can be mobilised through appropriate reorganisation of the economic system for constructional work without competing with the production of consumption goods. Subsequently, as the capital equipment under construction comes into operation it will have the positive effect of facilitating consumption: new sources of power or new technical equipment will raise the productivity of labour already engaged in the production of consumer goods.[22]

'When economic planning in the Soviet Union got underway there was already a sizeable agricultural surplus, and the task facing the planners was the diversion of this to the towns and industrial centres.'[23]

Paul Baran argues: 'If there were no other powerful reasons for the desirability of collectivisation of agriculture, the vital need for the mobilisation of the economic surplus generated in agriculture would in itself render collectivisation indispensable . . . Collectivisation destroys the basis for the peasants' resistance to the "siphoning off" of the economic surplus.'[24]

In other words, surplus resources in agriculture should be used as a source of capital construction, and a condition of success in this process is fundamental agrarian reorganisation. In the case of the Soviet Union, this reorganisation took the form of collectivisation.

The foundation of the first Five Year Plan was precisely its combination of plans for industrial development with a fundamental transformation of the agrarian system and of the traditional forms of rural economy. Measures for raising the productivity of labour in agriculture and at the same time for bringing the marketable surplus of agriculture more directly under planned control (by means of the so-called 'forward delivery contracts' which were to become obligatory supply quotas) had the effect of simultaneously releasing labour to swell the ranks of the industrial wage earners, reducing the number of mouths in the village and raising the productivity per man hour of labour on the land.[25]

The marketable surplus of agriculture that existed in the USSR in the 1920s, as it does today in much larger quantities in the underdeveloped countries (the causes behind this have been noted earlier), could be regarded as forming a 'fund of real working capital' for industrialisation. Investment of this working capital would cause rapid industrialisation, though the availability of this working capital requires reorganisation. In this sense, the Harrod-Domar growth theory, emphasising investment as the source of growth, is more applicable to such situations than the neoclassical approach to growth through development and technological change. Had Soviet Russian development been substantially based on imported capital and technology, it would have lessened the importance of agrarian reorganisation as a means for more productive utilisation of domestic resources, nor would such reorganisation have been required. The consequences would have been the frustration of the industrial revolution, stagnation in agriculture and the persistence of a dualistic structure of the economy, as happened in China during its first Five Year Plan (see Chapter 6), and in underdeveloped countries today where imported industrialisation is proving an insurmountable stumbling block to development.

However, in Soviet Russia during the industrialisation debate an intense controversy arose concerning the above notion of the source of real working capital as the crucial limiting factor. According to this view, any increase of investment must be preceded by an enlargement of the agricultural surplus otherwise the pace of industrialisation would be slow. In Dobb's view

> this fund was not necessarily a limiting factor in the sense that its prior enlargement was an essential condition for more investment at least so far as food supplies were concerned. A different distribution of grain between village and industrial areas was needed when rural labour was mobilised for industrial construction, the former becoming the consumers of food in the town instead of in the village. As a consequence, neither the volume of total consumption nor the consumption per head of population remaining in the village were necessarily reduced. Moreover, if changes were simultaneously introduced into the economic and social life of the village which simultaneously released both labour and mouths from the village and raised the productivity of the labour remaining there a growth of industrial investment could be accompanied by an actual growth in total consumption.[26]

But undoubtedly the success of this process essentially depends upon the economic reorganisation and planning. In this sense, industrial revolution in the twentieth century requires as a pre-condition for its success state control and direction of the means of production and distribution of resources. The industrial revolution in China basically followed this path. This will be discussed in the following chapter.

The brief account that we have given of the Russian economic situation reveals that Russia faced the problems of unemployment, surplus rural labour, a regressive agrarian structure and consequently a low standard of living. The only way to meet these problems was a rapid industrialisation of the country to absorb the surplus population as well as to raise the level of their productivity. We have also noted that the course of industrialisation became the subject of a long debate at that time. The debate centred broadly round three questions of policy:

(1) Whether to lay the primary emphasis on agriculture.
(2) Whether to achieve rapid industrialisation which would then stimulate agricultural development.
(3) Whether industrialisation should be based on foreign capital.

According to one school,

To conclude that we should be able to extract enough capital for the development of our extinct industry from taxation would be to console ourselves with hollow illusions. To flatter ourselves that we could raise this capital 'out of pennies' would be to add to the old delusion another . . . The government should take energetic steps to raise the necessary means by foreign and internal state loans and by granting concessions with greater loss and greater sacrifice than the state is prepared to take on itself for granting credits. Great material sacrifices for international capital, which is prepared to build up our industry, would be a lesser evil than the condition into which we might drift in the next few years.[27]

According to this school, peasant agriculture was to be stimulated by extensive concessions, even if this led to the rise of petty capitalism in the countryside. In this connection, a policy of 'good intervention' had been canvassed, i.e. village markets were to be supplied with large-scale imports of consumer goods from abroad to supplement the deficient supplies that home industry was able to furnish, and thereby increase the turnover between village and town. This school thought that the simultaneous development of industry and agriculture was impossible and this problem could not be solved without large imports of capital or a sudden forcible takeover of agriculture.[28] Contrary to the 'dictatorship of industry' school, Shannin advocated that agricultural development should be given the first priority, since Russian industry could only expand on the basis of imported equipment, the importation of which would only become possible on the basis of an enlarged surplus of agricultural produce for export. Professor Kondriatev, who was the author of a Five Year Plan for 1923-8 issued by the Commissariat of Agriculture of the Russian Republic, stated that 'at the centre of attention everywhere stands the creation of a rationalised agriculture'. He advocated generous financial assistance to the peasant economy and greater freedom for land leases and the hiring of labour by well-to-do peasants.[29]

According to another school of thought which laid emphasis on agriculture, expansion and improvement of the efficiency of agriculture should be treated as prerequisites for the industrialisation programme.[30] A prosperous agriculture was necessary to ensure an adequate flow of raw materials and food to the expanding industrial sector and also to provide a market for industry as it expanded. In this view only a prosperous peasantry could provide such a market.

Opponents to this view emphasised the idea that rapid industrialisation calling for investment on a broad front was essential to get the economy over the hump and started on the path of rapid economic growth.[31] Closely associated with this view was the idea that if industrialisation was to be completely successful, the planners would have to use the latest developments in technology. For instance, electricity would have to be used to provide the motive power for industry, very large specialised plants would have to be built and equipped with the most modern technology. That is, industry was to be made highly capital-intensive to make it very productive. In this view, producers' goods industries were to be made quite capital-intensive compared to consumer goods industries. The position of this school regarding the source of finance for this industrialisation programme was that tremendous savings (i.e. surplus in the form of labour, food and raw materials) would have to be mobilised from the agricultural sector. And this could be successful only if agriculture was reorganised to release the above resources for the industrialisation programmes. Thus a policy of collectivisation in agriculture to make surplus available for rapid industrialisation on the basis of the 'producers' goods industries first' principle was undertaken, and initiated the first industrial revolution of the twentieth century.

Economic Reorganisation

The twentieth-century cases of industrial revolution are different from the classical case of industrial revolution in the nineteenth century. Table 1.1 indicates the basic differences between the two. Professor Dobb, a leading authority on Soviet economic development, wrote that the economic development of Soviet Russia 'affords a unique example of the transformation of a formerly backward country to a country of extensive industrialisation and modern technique at an unprecedented tempo; a transformation unaffected by any considerable import of capital from abroad but effected under the guidance and control of a national economic plan instead of in the conditions of laissez-faire and atomistic capitalist enterprises which characterised the industrial revolutions of the past'. He further observed that 'the process of industrial revolution seems likely in turn to become the classic type for the future industrialisation of the countries of Asia'.[32]

In Soviet Russia the industrial revolution took the form of effecting fundamental changes in the agrarian economic structure to release resources to be used for capital formation, initially in the industrial sector, and subsequently in the agricultural sector. The mobilisation of resources from the largest sector needed this reorganisation. Agricultural collectivisation achieved its primary objective of sharply increasing the marketed proportion to total output. Between 1928 and 1932, sales of grain to state procurement agencies doubled and then doubled again during the second plan.[33] The marketed share of the grain crop rose from 15 to

40 per cent between 1928 and 1939.[34] Although the Kulaks'[35] rebellion in opposition to collectivisation led to a decline in grain output by ten per cent during 1928-32, the slaughter of draught animals by the Kulaks led to a sharp fall in animal power which was alleviated by a crash programme of agricultural machinery production and imports. Thus the horse population between 1928 and 1932 was reduced from 35.5 to 16.6 million. During this period, the stock of tractors rose more than eight-fold, from 26.7 to 210.7 thousand. During the following six years the stock of tractors more than doubled and the number of farm trucks multiplied some eight times.[36]

The increased mechanisation after 1932 enabled agricultural output to exceed pre-collectivisation levels by 1937. This led to a large increase in the marketed share and a recovery of living standards in rural areas.[37] Thus agriculture through collectivisation was able to supply the industrial sector with resources, human and natural (i.e. food and raw materials). A part of the latter was exported to pay for the imports of capital goods and in return agriculture received increased productive inputs to supplement the loss of labour to urban areas as well as to give effect to large-scale agriculture resulting from collectivisation. Rural labour was drawn in large numbers to urban occupations which were paid competitive wages in the high priority industrial sectors. Between 1928 and 1940 average earnings in coal mining rose from the fourteenth to first position among Soviet industrial sectors, in ferrous metallurgy from ninth to second, and in petroleum from eighth to third. In contrast, the earnings rank of footwear dropped from fourth to ninth and clothing from seventh to thirteenth.[38] The turnover ratio, the proportion of workers hired to annual average employment, rose from 100.8 per cent in 1928 to 176.4 per cent by 1932. Obviously, the ratio began to show a declining trend and had dropped below 100 per cent by 1935.[39]

Within twelve years collectivisation and organised recruitment reduced the proportion of the labour force depending on agriculture by 20 per cent from 71 to 51 per cent between 1928 and 1940. The shift was far more rapid than in the other major economies, with shifts of comparable proportions requiring 60 years in France, 65 years in Italy, 40 in the United States and 30 to 35 in Japan. However, it is to be noted that collectivisation led to an increase in productive employment in rural areas of 2.4 million between 1928 and 1934 and by another four million between 1937 and 1940, which might be explained as partly due to the growth in population.

The large resources mobilised through economic reorganisation were used to increase investment for capital construction as well as for importing technology from the West to make the resources more productive. In Soviet Russia this importation of technology did not lead to the problems that China faced during her first Five Year Plan (see Chapter 6) for the following reasons: (i) the labour supply was small compared to the need for very rapid growth;[40] (ii) the technology imported from the West had been relatively less capital-intensive than it became in the 1950s; (iii) the proportion of imported technology and capital to the total economic activity was very small, foreign trade as a proportion of GNP being only 3.5 per cent; (iv) these foreign resources were earned through the increased productivity of domestic resources – rural and urban – unlike what happened in China in the 1950s and is happening in other underdeveloped countries today; (v) these foreign resources were used not for building up consumer goods industries but for building up producers' goods industries. Investment got priority over consumption in the Soviet plan for industrialisation. Within the aggregate of industrial production the output of industrial raw materials and producers' goods rose much more rapidly than that of consumer goods, including home-processed food and clothing.

Compared with most industrialised countries, foreign trade has played a minor role in the USSR, as noted by Dobb. It was nevertheless important in some respects. We noted before that foreign investment and technology played the vital role in the Tsarist period of industrialisation. On the eve of the Soviet Revolution, exports accounted for ten per cent of GNP. Almost twelve per cent of the grain crop, 25 per cent of lumber and twelve per cent of petroleum were exported while machinery and textile raw materials comprised one-third of imports.

In the Soviet period, i.e. by 1930, the ratio of exports to GNP had risen to 3.5 per cent from almost non-existent in the years immediately after the revolution, a proportion which it has not reached again since that date. Agricultural products comprised nearly half of the total exports.[41] Imports included growth-oriented products. Thus in the early 1930s machinery and ferrous metal amounted to nearly 75 per cent of total imports. Imports were also the overwhelming source of supply of key non-ferrous metals. Since the second Five Year Plan the Soviet leadership have pursued a policy of autonomy for the development of domestic productive capabilities in machinery and metals and thus the foreign trade volume fell absolutely as well as relative to the national product.

In conclusion, Soviet Russia's economic development was essentially a case of the twentieth-century process of industrial revolution, which is based on indigenous resources mobilised for more productive utilisation through fundamental changes in economic organisation. Changes in economic organisation substituted the process of capital formation. Imported modern technology (though as a proportion to GNP it was negligible) played an important role, but the development was essentially a result of the more productive utilisation of domestic resources. We can therefore say that the industrial revolution that led to self-sustained growth in Soviet Russia was essentially a function of economic reorganisation that released resources and made possible their more productive use. It was, however, a socially planned approach. In this sense the first case of twentieth-century industrial revolution differs from the classical one of the nineteenth century. But in essence both processes are the same in the sense that both processes resulted from the increasing pressure of population on existing resources, necessitating technological changes which in turn required fundamental changes in the socio-economic and political structures of the country.

Notes

1. M. Dobb, *Soviet Economic Development since 1917* (Routledge and Kegan Paul, London, 1948), p. 39.

2. Ibid., Ch. I for a detailed discussion of this aspect.

3. Ibid., p. 24.

4. Ibid., p. 39.

5. Ibid., p. 40.

6. Ibid., p. 42.

7. Ibid., pp. 34-60 for a detailed discussion of agricultural conditions prior to the First World War.

8. J.P. McKay, 'Foreign Entrepreneurship in Russian Industrialisation', *Journal of Economic History*, no. 26 (1966), pp. 582-3.

9. B. Higgins, *Economic Development* (Constable and Co., London, 1959), section on technological dualism.

10. Dobb, *Soviet Economic Development*, p. 34.

11. Ibid., p. 34.

12. Ibid., p. 35.

13. Ibid., p. 36.

14. Ibid., pp. 34-5.

15. W. Parker, *Journal of Economic History*, no. 25 (1965), p. 38.

16. H.J. Ellison, *Journal of Economic History*, no. 25 (1965), p. 538.

17. Ibid., p. 539.

18. S.O. Zagorsky, *State Control of Industry in Russia during the War* (Yale University Press, 1928), p. 16.

19. Ellison, p. 539.

20. Dobb, *Soviet Economic Development*, p. 12.

21. Ibid., p. 13.

22. Ibid., p. 14.

23. W.H. Nicholls, 'The Place of Agriculture in Economic Development' in C.K. Eicher and L.W. Witt (eds.), *Agriculture in Economic Development* (FAO, 1964).

24. P. Baran, *The Political Economy of Growth* (Monthly Review Press, New York, 1962), p. 268; J.R. Millar and A. Nove, 'Agricultural Surplus Hypothesis', *Soviet Studies*, no. 22 (1970-1).

25. Dobb, *Soviet Economic Development*, p. 25.

26. Ibid., p. 24.

27. Medvediev, Letter to Baku (in Baku Group), 1924 (cf. Dobb, p. 200).

28. L. Shannin, *Bolshevik*, no. 2 (1926), p. 70; Dobb, *Soviet Economic Development*, p. 207.

29. Dobb, *Soviet Economic Development*, p. 20.

30. R.W. Campbell, *The Great Industrialisation Debate in Soviet Economic Power* (Houghton Mifflin, Boston, 1966), pp. 8-28; S.H. Cohn, *Economic Development in the Soviet Union* (Heath and Co., 1970), pp. 18-25; Dobb, *Soviet Economic Development*, pp. 177-208.

31. Dobb, *Soviet Economic Development*, p. 2.

32. Ibid., p. 2.

33. A. Baykov, *The Development of the Soviet Economic System* (Cambridge University Press, 1946), p. 326.

34. N. Jasny, *Socialised Structure of the USSR Food Research Institute* (Stanford, 1959), p. 794.

35. Kulaks were defined as those who hired outside labour or rented out farm equipment. 'Poor' peasants were defined as those without draft animals and cultivating no more than 2.6 acres.

36. H. Schwartz, *Russia's Soviet Economy* (Prentice Hall, 1958), p. 539.

37. S.H. Cohn, *Economic Development in the Soviet Union* (Heath, 1970), p.34.

38. Ibid.

39. Baykov, *Development*, p. 215.

40. Evaluated in 1928 prices, the GNP growth between 1928 and 1937 was very high – 11.9 per cent per annum. The Soviet population had grown quite slowly at a rate of one half of one per cent per annum. See A. Bergson, *The Real National Income of Soviet Russia since 1928* (Harvard University Press, 1961).

41. F. Holzman, 'Foreign Trade' in A. Bergson and S. Kuznets (eds.), *Economic Trends in the Soviet Union* (Harvard University Press, 1963), p. 232.

6 INDUSTRIAL REVOLUTION IN THE TWENTIETH CENTURY: CHINA

Introduction

We have noticed from our study of the effects of the pressure of population on patterns of development in the nineteenth century that the main trend in that period was a product of a combination of three economic factors. The need to raise productivity due to the growing pressure of population-initiated technological change, innovations and inventions which necessitated organisational change (including changes in production relations in terms of the abolition of serfdom and feudalism) so that resources lying idle and/or malutilised in the existing economic organisation could be released to give effect to innovations and other technological changes. This in turn caused further changes in technology and thus gave birth to a dynamic force resulting in the industrial revolution. In the case of Germany, France or Japan, organisational change in agriculture (e.g. abolishing serfdom etc.) was initiated to release resources to earn foreign technology, capital and skill to develop the modern industrial sector, which, however, was not intended for agricultural development nor resulted from the increase in agricultural productivity of these countries. We have already noticed the consequences of such industrialisation in Chapter 2. The latter cases of the imported industrialisation process in a free enterprise economic framework could be described in terms of classical models of growth as interpreted by Lewis, Fei and Ranis.[1] Output in these models is considered as dependent on the classical production function, i.e. demand for and supply of labour is determined by the real wage, and any increase in the supply of labour causing wages to fall would be automatically absorbed, leading to further growth. In this process of growth, the rate of capital formation has been augmented, accompanied by an increasing demand for labour. But in developed countries the population growth rate has slowed down since the early twentieth century for reasons stated earlier and as a consequence, the rate of capital formation far exceeded the level of labour supply, which necessitated a change in further emphasis, to the technological change. Neoclassicists[2] took up this issue and developed their model, the implications of which for labour-surplus underdeveloped countries will be discussed later.

Before we take it up we have to refer to the Keynesian model for short-term fluctuations as developed by Harrod and Domar for long-term growth problems. This model has been used as the basis for many development plans (e.g. the second Indian Five Year Plan).

A crucial question needs discussion in the light of modern Western growth theories — Keynesian and neoclassical, the analysis of the role of investment and technological change in labour-surplus economies, including China in its initial stage of development.

The early Keynesian model, which focused on the problem of short-term stability in an economy, treated investment as a component of effective aggregate demand. This demand component was so volatile in a market economy that its fluctuation tended to cause depressions or inflation if it was not offset by a proper compensatory policy of the government. Domar emphasised the dual role of investment as a demand-creating factor and capacity-creating factor on the supply side. On this is based the modern Keynesian growth theory as developed by Harrod and Domar in their models.[3]

Thereafter investment became the most important element in all growth and development models. In this view increased investment leads to full employment. However, under full employment conditions further capacity-creation through increased investment would result in the operation of the law of diminishing returns. What was needed was to increase the productivity of the existing resources through the encouragement of technological change. This was a neoclassical stand. The importance of investment rested essentially on the capacity-creating factor and this is of crucial importance to a labour-short economy, while in an underdeveloped country, although the capacity-creating factor has the most dominant place in development, attempts to create capacity with the help of foreign resources are failing to generate demand-effects, i.e. the other side of the model. In a developed full-employment economy, there is the problem of demand created through increased investment. During recession these economies face this problem because of the fall in investment. Investment is thus the crucial factor.

Another important contribution in recent times has been made by R.M. Solow,[4] who built his model of growth on the classical concept known as the neoclassical growth model. It assumes full employment at all times as did the classicists of the nineteenth century. Therefore, the demand-creating function of investment has very little significance as we mentioned earlier. The model is essentially based on the other aspect of investment, i.e. the capacity-increasing side. According to Solow's calculation based on American 'historical data' the contribution of investment to economic growth is of far less significance than that of technological change. His results showed that 87 per cent of the increase in output per unit of labour input came from technological progress and only 13 per cent stemmed from the expansion of capital stock.

Solow's study obviously is not applicable even to other developed countries of the day. The modern sector of the USA, since its very inception with the coming of the migrants from Europe, faced a labour shortage and hence growth required rapid technological change to make imported technology more capital-intensive so as to substitute labour, unlike in the UK.[5]

Habakkuk's explanation of the phenomenon is very valuable. In his opinion the basic explanation for this difference stemmed from the fact that American businessmen were perpetually short of labour. Labour scarcity encouraged a search for labour-saving innovations – a search which met little opposition from organised labour unions because it did not threaten the displacement of workers by machines (on the contrary it was likely to result in an increase in the aggregate demand for labour, and a general rise in the level of real wages). Technical progress in one sector of the economy stimulated similar innovations in other sectors, the more so in the American case since any sectoral rise in real wages due to technical progress put pressure on other branches of the economy to introduce labour-saving equipment in order to prevent a drain of higher paid employment. In other words, investment to improve technology with a view to using existing resources more productively has played the dominant role in growth. Furthermore, the labour shortage, causing higher wages, caused a downward pressure on profit as well as adversely affecting business interests in the international market. American businessmen had to introduce capital-saving technology in order to economise on the rising real costs of other factors of production. In contrast, in England, where labour was in adequate supply, the adoption of labour-saving machinery was not immediately needed, and in addition England had the advantage of a vast competition-free market of colonies.

In the case of England the slow growth of technology compared to the USA and Germany, for example, may be explained by the fact that the UK had an assured and vast market for her products initially in other parts of Europe and then in the colonies where the UK enjoyed a protected market. Obviously, she had to face little competition and hence the motivation to achieve efficiency was lacking. In the case of the USA, Germany or Japan, to get a foothold and then to expand in the world market required from the very beginning a motivation to improve efficiency to compete with others, which may explain the superiority of efficiency in technology achieved by these countries.

One criticism of Solow's initial model was that the measured contribution of technological changes is really a residual which reflects the working of all economic forces other than the inputs of labour and capital. Moreover, the importance of investment is understated because the model assumes that all technological changes have been disembodied from production. Yet in reality the majority of innovations have to be embodied in new machines and equipment, and the gains from these innovations cannot be realised unless firms make investments. This last point led Solow to develop his vintage model of economic growth, in which the embodiment effect of investment is taken into consideration.[6] However, even in this new model the contribution of investment to economic growth is overshadowed by other factors.

The importance of investment cannot be ignored because it is such a vital component in aggregate demand. In an affluent society investment must take place at a high rate if effective demand is to be maintained with full employment.

In China, investment has played a very important role. Its importance, however, does not lie on the demand side. The crucial role of investment is on the supply side, i.e. through more productive utilisation of underutilised resources. Institutional change in this respect plays the role of capital formation. It played this role in China in her industrial revolution and also in Europe at the time of industrialisation in the last century. Solow's model is not applicable to China or to underdeveloped countries today where there is surplus labour, i.e. the person whose marginal product falls below the minimum subsistence cost. The bulk of surplus labour exists in the rural areas where farmers share their output among family members. The marginal productivity of surplus labour is so low because the existing stock of capital goods is not sufficient to match the labour force. According to modern economics, only investment can provide extra employment opportunities in the urban areas and absorb unused labour productively. The source of investment, whether indigenous or external, is of course of importance. If the source is indigenous it is generated by changes in economic organisation. But the recent experience of underdeveloped countries and that of China in the 1950s show that increased investment from external sources can help in achieving a high rate of growth but do little for employment opportunities. Investment based on indigenous resources can create adequate employment opportunities but its mobilisation requires basic changes in economic organisation to release resources for investment in the desired sectors. In China in the first Five Year Plan both steps were taken, i.e.

investment was augmented and the economy was reorganised. But there remained a fly in the ointment, i.e. investment in the industrial sector was largely based on imported inputs which led to serious imbalance in the economy in the subsequent period.

Where the amount of surplus labour is exceedingly large, as it is in China and the UDCs, the absorption of unused labour outweighs the embodiment of technological changes as the primary source of economic growth. Technology change evolves in the process of making indigenous resources more productive. This needs, as a basic condition, changes in economic organisation. In other words, output is increased at a higher rate by putting increased labour into production rather than by raising the productivity of those who are already employed through borrowed technology and capital, which is the result of an increased productivity of resources elsewhere. That is, investment can fulfil its role of increasing demand through increased productivity of resources i.e. supply. We are back to the classical situation of supply creating its own demand.

Unfortunately, there is a conflict between the embodiment of technical changes and the absorption of unused labour in the present-day world. In other words, supply today does not create its own demand if the supply is not the result of the utilisation of domestic resources. The new machines and production techniques developed by the advanced labour-short economies, including the Soviet Union, tend to be labour saving. Direct borrowing of modern technology from these countries would generate a minimum employment opportunity per unit of investment. This is clearly demonstrated by the experience of China in its first Five Year Plan and of underdeveloped countries since the beginning of the development decade. The latter countries could not escape the disastrous effects of such investment policies until today, while China changed its strategy and thus was able to avoid them.

China's Economy on the Eve of her Industrial Revolution

Chinese economic development since the 1950s, i.e. since the foundation of the People's Republic, may be classified as a case of an industrial revolution of the mid-twentieth century. The pre-revolution period in China's economy is characterised by dualism with a small modern sector based on foreign capital and technology and a large traditional agricultural sector comprising 80 per cent of the total population. A very large proportion of the country was generally considered uncultivatable (nearly 90 per cent of the area of Greater China, and about 70 per cent of China proper). Because of the pressure of population a considerably larger part of the potentially fertile land was brought into cultivation. The proportion actually in use was estimated in the 1930s as 27 per cent of the area of China proper (i.e. 240 to 250 million acres), i.e. 90 per cent of potentially fertile land.[7] The constant population pressure, and the perpetual fragmentation of the land through the centuries as a result of the Chinese laws of inheritance had by the 1930s provided an average farm of about 3.31 acres compared with one of 39.74 in Denmark, 77.3 acres in England and Wales and 156 to 185 acres in the USA.[8] This small size of the average farm in China was further reduced in the next 25 years. However, the soil of China, after some thousands of years of cultivation, has, through the intensive use of natural fertiliser, still retained much of its fertility. In some areas though, there were problems of erosion caused by denudation of vegetation, taken for fuel, fodder and fertiliser.[9] J.L. Bulk wrote: 'The main Chinese crops were those directly usable for human consumption, particularly grains (mainly wheat and rice) and beans. Soya beans are the most important— a food resource of great versatility, which can be used for human and animal food, for oil or for manufacturing purposes. Pressure of population has made it necessary to produce the greatest amount of food possible per unit of land. Yields were very low despite the high intensity of labour. The average pre-war yield of wheat was 9.7 quintals per hectare compared with 21.2 in Britain and 33.1 in Denmark and even rice yields were significantly lower than in Japan, though higher than in India.'[10]

Some important commercial crops like cotton, silk, tea, tungoil and tobacco were also produced. These were partly used domestically and partly sold for cash.

The Chinese methods of cultivation and implements were mostly primitive. Wooden ploughs were common in China in the 1930s. The Chinese economy has been marked by a great growth of population; it doubled between the seventeenth and nineteenth centuries. In the middle of the nineteenth century it was estimated at about 340 million. By the 1930s the population had increased to a figure of 450-500 million. This huge growth of population has been the result of a long period of internal peace, the introduction of new crops and an expansion of the cultivated area, as mentioned by many economists.[11] The urban population constituted only 20 per cent of the whole.

According to the Nationalist Government figures, due to intense pressure of population as mentioned earlier, the average division of cultivatable area per head of the farm population was of about two thirds of an acre. More recent estimates suggest that the present average may be only about half an acre.[12] The land ownership pattern was revealed by an investigation carried out in rural China in the 1930s, which showed that about 50 per cent of the farmers owned the land they worked, just under 33 per cent were part owners and about 17 per cent were tenants.[13] These were, however, regional variations. Rents were normally very high, varying from 50 to 75 per cent of the produce. Under the circumstances, farms were excessively fragmented and scattered, with an average farm of just over three acres and divided into five or six separate strips, with a distance of nearly half a mile between farmhouse and strips. The size of farms was marked by considerable inequalities as the following figures show. 36 per cent of the farms were under 1.7 acres, and 25 per cent were between 1.7 and 3.4.[14]

These types of economies are characterised by the predominance of small-scale traditional industries. China's traditional industries were normally organised in units smaller than those known during the Roman empire or in medieval Europe. Many were carried out by the individual within the home unlike in Europe where many goods like clothes, furniture and other household objects were made by specialist craftsmen or in workshops.

The largest-scale industry was salt mining. There were tin, iron and coal mines but none of these commodities were used to the extent that they have been in Europe. Gold, silver and copper were mined for use in currency and ornaments as in other Eastern countries. There were industries to produce luxury goods for the use of the imperial courts and small wealthy urban classes. The most flourishing of these manufacturing industries were the porcelain, brocade, enamel ware, lacquer, ivory and jade ware industries. These craft industries were organised into guilds similar to those which existed in medieval Europe. There were also cottage industries run by the peasant women and some peasants in subsidiary occupations. These were sericulture, basket work, weaving, embroidery and pottery industries meant for poorer consumers, including the better off among the villagers themselves and townspeople who could not always afford the products of the luxury industries mentioned above.

Modern industries in China are of very recent origin, and mostly based on Western and Japanese capital. China was opened to Western trade under the Treaty of Nanking of 1842 and for the first time the methods of large-scale commercial organisations and modern financial institutions were introduced at this time to meet the demand for Western trade. But after about 50 years, under the Treaty of Shimonesiki of 1895, foreign industrial enterprises were permitted to operate and this immediately resulted in the establishment of foreign-owned cotton mills and other factories at the ports, mainly in Shanghai. Financed by foreign capital, a network of railways linking the main ports of China was established to serve the Western trading interests. The most important railway systems were built by the Russians in North Manchuria and by the Japanese in South Manchuria.[15]

The revolution of 1911 and the subsequent period of political uncertainties culminating in war between China and Japan in 1937 were not very encouraging to foreign investment. But the important foreign privileges, the foreign settlements and extra-territorial rights were not abandoned by the major Western powers until towards the end of the Second World War.

Foreign-owned industries constituted the modern sector in the Chinese economy, as was usual in all the underdeveloped countries of the period. Industries were largely concentrated on the Treaty ports and along the Yangtse Valley, which revealed another fundamental truth about the process of imported industrialisation of the period, i.e. industries grew not to serve the needs of the indigenous economy but those of the industrialised nations. Even for light industrial goods the country was dependent on imports for between 50 and 70 per cent of requirements. In 1937 only about nine per cent of the industrial resources of China proper could be classified as capital industry, including communications, construction, water and electricity supply, metallurgy, brick works etc. These were mostly foreign owned.[16]

Modern industrial growth based on foreign capital is geared to foreign trade and needs a well-developed transport and communication system. Thus in China proper by 1937 there were about 7,000 miles of railways, airlines linked the major cities and highway mileage increased from 20,000 in 1927 to 75,000 in 1937. In Shanghai, Tientsin, and Hangkow there was a fairly rapid development of modern foreign-owned businesses. Employment in industry was over a million (i.e. almost 0.2 per cent of the total population), while about ten million more were engaged in handicrafts.[17]

But the most important industrial growth on Chinese soil was due to the Japanese in Formosa and in Manchuria where they developed a flourishing heavy industry complex. In 1937, about half the coal, about two thirds of the iron and something like 90 per cent of the steel produced in China came from Manchuria. There was very little development of heavy industry in China proper where such modern industry as had developed was almost entirely light industry, especially textiles, which accounted for nearly half the total industrial output. The total output of steel outside Manchuria was only 50,000 tons, of pig iron 430,000 tons, and of coal 20 million tons.[18] In other words, a modern sector was developed in Formosa, leaving China proper as an underdeveloped hinterland with few diffusion effects, as was the case with the limited impact of imported modern investment in other countries of the Third World in the comparable period.

Obviously, indigenous capital resources were scarce. The small Chinese businesses that existed were mainly run as personal and family concerns.

This is a brief account of an underdeveloped China facing increasing pressure of population with a low standard of living and low productivity in the traditional sector, which comprised nearly 80 per cent of the economy, and a small imported modern sector geared to the needs of foreign trade which had not evolved to meet the need of utilising domestic resources more productively.

With this outline in mind, we will discuss the process of the industrial revolution that was carried out by the People's Republic of China from the 1950s. There are three stages in this process, which were meant to correct the mistakes of earlier stages.

In the first stage, with a view to securing a high growth rate, China laid great emphasis on the industrial sector. In this approach more productive foreign capital and technology play the dominant role. In the case of China, Soviet investment and transplantation of capital and technology played that role in the first Five Year Plan (1952-6). In development as well as in reorganisation of the agrarian economic structure the Soviet strategy of collectivisation was followed. It resulted in a very rapid growth of modern industries but in the stagnation of agriculture. This is discussed in detail below.

In the second stage, a policy of 'walking with two legs' was pursued, i.e. a deliberate policy of industrial dualism was initiated with emphasis both on the expansion of modern industries based mainly on foreign capital, largely from the Soviet Union, and on raising agricultural output with the help of labour-intensive methods so that the total output of the economy could be raised. But it created a serious divergence in terms of income and productivity distribution between the two sectors, and the agricultural sector being the largest sector comprising 80 per cent of the population suffered most.

The formation of the communes appears to be the basic organisational change introduced to bring about an agricultural revolution resulting in the growth of indigenous technology and leading to the industrial revolution.

Fundamental change in agrarian organisation to mobilise surplus labour in rural areas cannot lead to agricultural revolution if the industrial sector is based on foreign resources. The following review of China's policy of economic development will prove the contention.

The Process of China's Industrial Revolution

In the twentieth-century cases of the industrial revolution, mobilisation and utilisation of surpluses could not be left to the individual's choice entirely for economic reasons. The state undertook this responsibility and thus minimised serious barriers to domestic saving and mobilised a maximum amount of surplus for economic development. These obstacles were essentially institutional, e.g. the income inequality, feudal economic structure and faulty pattern of production and consumption that character-ise their pre-industrial revolution days.

According to the modern theory of economic growth, capital formation is considered to be constrained by peoples' low propensity to save. This is a problem in a private enterprise, class-divided society. But when the state controls all means of production and distribution, and thus sets prices and wages, private consumption is subject to direct government control. In other words, within a reasonable time the low propensity to save no longer forms a constraint because the government has the power to mobilise compulsory savings. The reason is that in this system the propensity to consume has little significance because of the subsistence level of income of the majority of the population and thus the 'keeping up with the Joneses' attitude is confined to a very small proportion of the people. A free enterprise economy survives and thrives through the effects of its ever increasing diversification of production and con-sumption which for its success requires income inequalities to generate and sustain the attitude of 'keeping up with the Joneses'.

The Chinese communists initially followed the 'walking with two legs' strategy for raising productivity in addition to capital formation. It is to be noted here that the Chinese communists, although they laid emphasis on the expansion of capital in the non-agricultural sector, at the same time introduced institutional changes in the sector. For the non-agricultural sector, they laid emphasis on the expansion of capital investment as the means of raising productivity and output, and for agriculture the communists hoped to promote productivity and output through institutional changes with a minimum amount of capital invest-ment. This approach is different from the Soviet one in the sense that Soviet planners followed agricultural collectivisation as a policy to mobilise resources from the largest sector in order to finance its industrial sector, which in turn was expected to help promote productivity in the agricultural sector. The factor-endowment situation in Soviet Russia at the initial period of the industrial revolution (i.e. a relatively small population compared to a vast land area, and a relatively large industrial sector, though based on imported resources during pre-1917 days), as well as the need for rapid growth and a defence build-up, being the first socialist country, made the Russian industrial revolution process somewhat different, although basically the industrial revolutions of the nineteenth and twentieth centuries are the same in the sense that industrial development in both cases ensued from the increased productivity of agriculture. In other words, investment in all cases of industrial revolution is a function of organisational changes to make resources more productive. In the case of China, vast human resources were considered as a great asset in building up the economy. Both countries needed fundamental changes in economic organisation and production relations as a pre-condition for mobilising resources for development which were previously lying underutilised. This was, however, the basic condition for all industrial revolutions – both classic and twentieth-century ones.

The Chinese, under the influence of Soviet policy, initially introduced collective farming with a view to mobilising and utilising the existing resources more efficiently. Consequently, institutional changes could serve as a substitute for capital investment in the countryside. Institutional changes played the role of a substitute for capital investment in the classic Industrial Revolution as well as in cases of industrialisation without an industrial revolution in the nineteenth century.

In the cases of attempted industrialisation without an industrial revolution in the twentieth century this fundamental factor in economic development is absent. One economic reason which may be advanced for this absence is that these economies are provided with unlimited supplies of capital, technology and skill and consequently they do not need any such fundamental institutional changes to release resources for capital formation and technological change. This has led to tremendous growth in industrial output but obviously with little use of the domestic human resources which have remained underdeveloped.

But we will see that the Chinese approach of collectivisation to mobilise resources for industry to attain a higher industrial growth rate failed in generating an overall and integrated development process.

In the case of Soviet Russia, the policy of collectivisation worked for three economic reasons: (i) The factor-endowment situation, i.e. the supply of labour was not as plentiful compared to the need for rapid and overall development as it was in China; (ii) the technology used in the modern sector was not as capital-intensive at the time of industrial development in Russia as it was in China in the 1950s, where most was made available from Soviet Russia; (iii) the industrial sector was mainly geared to the production of capital goods, the supply of which to the rural economy helped in raising the productivity of the agricultural sector, thus enabling it to supply food, natural resources and human resources for the industrial sector. This has been achieved through institutional changes.

What happened in China?

In pre-communist days in China, as elsewhere in underdeveloped countries, the modern factories that were established or expanding were predominantly producing light and consumer goods such as textiles, flour, cigarettes and matches etc. Needless to say, most of them were based on foreign investment.

In contrast, the policy of the Chinese communists, during the first Five Year Plan following the Stalin model, accorded the highest priority to the production of producers' goods. Table 6.1 indicates the type of investment that characterised this period.

Table 6.1: Indicators of Industrial Growth in Mainland China, 1949-59
Industrial Production (1952=100)

Items	1949	1957	1959
Electric Power	60	266	572
Coal	49	195	523
Crude Petroleum	28	334	846
Steel Ingots	12	396	990
Metal-Cutting Machines	11	204	510
Railway Freight Cars	54	126	—
Bicycles	17	1001	1872
Spindles	—	126	365
Looms	—	—	338
Ammonium Sulphate	15	349	736
Sulphuric Acid	21	333	556
Caustic Soda	19	251	456
Tyres	62	209	—
Cement	23	240	429
Timber	51	249	368
Cotton Yarn	50	128	228
Manufactured Cotton Cloth	49	151	196
Paper	42	226	396
Sugar	44	191	250
Salt	60	167	223

Items	1949	1952	1959
Cigarettes	60	168	208
Vegetable Oil	45	112	149
Rubber Footwear	47	209	—
Matches	74	114	—
Total Industrial Product	—	246	385
Total Producer Goods Output	—	347	594
Total Consumption Goods Output	—	148	182

Source: these are values and aggregates based on estimates presented in T.C. Liu and K.C. Yeh, 'Preliminary Estimate of the National Income of the Chinese Mainland, 1952-59', *AER*, vol. 41, no. 2 (May 1961), p. 489.

The first detailed plan was formulated and implemented only after three years of economic rehabilitation. Towards the end of the first Five Year Plan (1955-7), a number of new problems arose which required a thorough review of current economic policy. The pace of investment and the emphasis on producing producers' goods became the subject matter of a great debate.

However, under the 'great leap forward' policy of 1958, a new feature, of planned industrial dualism, was introduced called the 'walking with two legs' policy. The chief idea was to obtain a greater increase in output with a given amount of new investment by building numerous small plants using indigenous and labour-intensive techniques of production.

This policy had serious repercussions for the whole economy. This investment policy led to serious imbalances—types of imbalances we are familiar with in underdeveloped countries. Serious imbalances were created between industry and agriculture, and between consumer goods and producers' goods within the industrial sector. (This aspect has been discussed earlier.)

The most disturbing feature of development in this period was the remarkable industrial growth relative to agricultural stagnation (see Table 6.1). David Mamo wrote that at the end of the 1950s the industrial, urban and coastal areas were characterised by a higher standard of living, higher vertical mobility and greater political power, and occupationally composed of specialised workers, intellectuals, and bureaucrats, and the rural and inland areas were characterised by a notably low standard of life, poor peasants and unskilled workers.[19]

The dualism, of a modern and rich industrial sector, and a poor traditional rural sector, that characterises today's underdeveloped countries was also evident at the initial period of the Chinese industrialisation

programme, when largely based on foreign resources. Tables 6.3 and 6.4
show the proportion of foreign aid to total investment in China. It is
evident that the industrial expansion was particularly rapid in producers'
goods, and intermediate goods industries, with consumer goods production
showing a considerable reduction of the rate of increase. However, total
industrial production seems to have grown at an average annual rate of
20 per cent during the first Five Year Plan, rising apparently even faster
in 1958-9, while the output of the producers' goods industries increased
even more rapidly, approximately by 30 per cent, and consumer goods
production appears to have gone up by less than ten per cent.[20]

In the case of private-sector-dominated underdeveloped countries, we
notice the opposite trend, i.e. the rate of growth of consumer goods
production is higher than that of the producers' goods industries (India's
second Five Year Plan results will bear this out). Yet the Chinese economy could not escape the trap of dualism, a result of industrialisation
based on foreign resources even though these largely came from another
socialist economy.

The rapid industrial growth was achieved by high rates of investment,
the bulk of which were channelled into expansion of the capacity of
producers' goods industries. While rates of investment averaged around
20 per cent during the first plan period, 56 per cent of this investment
total was allocated to the industrial sector, close to 90 per cent of which
was in turn devoted to raising producers' goods capacity. Transplantations of complete plant installations from Soviet Russia played a crucial
role in this significant rise in industrial productive capacity.

Over 80 per cent of the investment within the state plan in the first
Five Year Plan was allocated to heavy industry. Chao's estimates show
that investment in large plants accounted for more than 60 per cent of
the planned total investment.[21] Ordinarily, had these large modern plants
not been based on imported inputs, these would have created a chain of
employment through effects. Table 6.2 indicates the poor employment
effect of such investments.

Table 6.2

	Number ('000 persons)	Investment (1952=100)
1952	4,939	100
1953	6,188	125.3
1954	6,408	129.7
1955	6,477	131.1
1956	8,626	174.7
1957	9,008	182.4

Source: K. Chao, *Capital Formation in Mainland China, 1952-56* (University of California, 1974), p. 127.

According to official statistics, fixed assets of industrial enterprise increased by 123 per cent between 1952 and 1955 while industrial employment increased very slowly as the Table shows. It remained almost constant in 1953-5 despite the investment activities in that period. The net addition to employment due to investment under the first Five Year Plan was less than three million or about 30 per cent of the total number of industrial workers in 1957. There was a drastic rise in capital/labour ratio in that period.[22]

The relatively large increase in employment in 1953 must have been due to the rehabilitation work in the previous years in view of the preponderance of large-scale construction units in the investment plan. This was also the experience of most of the underdeveloped countries at the beginning of their economic development plans.

Even the three million additional jobs could not have been created had not the system of multiple shifts been applied to more and more enterprises. In some cases a system of four shifts each of eight working hours was introduced to avoid the slowing down of operation during the changing of shifts. It would not have been considered profitable in a free enterprise economy. China thus attempted to cut short the industrialisation process by socialisation. But despite this growth in industrialisation, the economy suffered from agricultural stagnation and problems of creating employment in the more productive sector, as indicated earlier.

The unusually rapid expansion in industrial capacity and high rates of industrial growth were largely made possible because of large Soviet aid in the form of new technology embodied in manufacturing equipment, machinery and installations of all types which could not be produced in China, new plant design and new scientific and technical knowledge. This was accompanied by imports of raw materials and semi-manufactured goods with some of which China was poorly endowed.

Some economists commented that China's experience would suggest that it would be no exaggeration to conclude that large-scale industrial imports made the difference between what in retrospect will undoubtedly turn out to be the country's industrial revolution or very slow growth. But this large industrial investment, mostly based on imported capital and other resources, was accompanied by a stagnating agriculture, the largest sector with nearly 80 per cent of the population depending on it. In other words, the expansion in the industrial sector did not come about through the increased productivity of the agricultural sector.

Obviously, in this circumstance, population growth creates a serious problem which led to a serious political controversy during this time in China's political and ideological leadership (particularly between Ma and Mao). This will be discussed later.

Rapid industrial growth can be attempted at the expense of agricultural development. This fact necessarily limited China's export capacity and therefore imports prior to 1955. This deficiency of agriculture was to some extent alleviated by sizeable foreign aid to China. This entire process is contrary to the process of an industrial revolution as discussed earlier. Underdeveloped countries today are facing identical problems of rapid industrial growth and stagnating overpopulated agriculture at the same time.

This question of overpopulation raised a stormy controversy in China as mentioned earlier. At the end of 1956 and during the first half od 1957 Ma Yin-Chiu, a leading economist and President of Peking University wrote: 'I consider that a high population with a low level of investment is a very serious consideration.'[23] He further wrote, 'China's population growth is too fast and capital accumulation seems to be too slow.'[24]

Ma advocated birth control as a necessary means of increasing the quality of the population and of helping to solve the problem of employment. Today we are very familiar with this line of argument in underdeveloped countries. This approach logically follows attempted industrialisation with imported capital and technology even though from one socialist country to another. Because this imported capital and technology came from labour-short countries, it did not create a demand for labour and as a consequence population was considered as the stumbling block to development.

The opposite view was expressed by Mao Tse Tung who did not belittle the high population in a country where only 20 per cent of the land is cultivatable but regarded it as the major asset in development.

He wrote: 'When we plan, carry out affairs, think about problems, we must start| from the fact that China has 600 million people and at all costs we must not overlook this point.' He urged six hundred million people to recognise this as an objective fact and that 'it is our *capital*. China's large population is a good thing, but, of course, it has its difficulties.'[25]

China under Mao introduced a new agrarian organisation in the later period, through the communes, with a view to making more productive use of human resources. The earlier policy of collectivisation proved inadequate. The communes, as we have noticed earlier, evolved from traditional land reforms policy through collectivisation. The role of the commune was not confined to agriculture but was also applied to industrial production in the rural sector. This policy led to a tremendous demand for labour and created a situation of labour shortage. Ma wrote: 'On the one hand, we have a picture of China studying how to utilise its labour fully and attempting all kinds of techniques of using labour more productively in order to do so, countering the agricultural underdevelopment associated with underdeveloped agrarian economies.'[26] On the other, Ma draws attention to the growing phenomenon of labour shortage in rural areas throughout China. He, however, does not discuss this in relation to the increasing demand for labour under the organisation of communes but in relation to the demand for labour by agriculture, especially when double cropping is attempted. He therefore suggested: 'The future key to the rich increases in rural production is in mechanical assistance during the excessively busy period.'[27] Ma gave more importance to material inputs than to organisational change as an alternative means of capital formation. Mao's policy was to use institutional changes as a substitute for capital investment.

However, investment accelerated at a very high rate during the early period of development, i.e. 1952-7. The average annual rate of fixed capital investment, that is, the proportion of GNP devoted to fixed capital formation, was 17.8 per cent in that period.[28] This is more than double the rate of 7.5 per cent for 1951-6.[29]

The Chinese and Soviet experiences show that the level of investment is a significant function of economic institutions. The rate of capital formation in pre-war China was obviously determined by the low level of voluntary saving in the private sector. The low level of income and the age structure of the population resulting from an extremely low life expectancy, as common in pre-industrial economies, were unfavourable to saving efforts. In addition we must take note of acute income inequality. The richer people belonging to the rentier and trading classes acted as a hindrance to capital formation. These groups usually indulged in conspicuous consumption met by imports in most cases. An extraordinarily large number of people were under the working age. Both the fertility rate and the infant mortality rate being very high, a demographic characteristic during pre-industrial days, a considerable amount of the economic surplus of society had to be wasted on raising children who did not survive to participate in productive work.

So far as capital formation is concerned the main change in the 1950s occurred in the mechanism for mobilising surplus resources.

The principal form this mechanism took was the direct use of surplus labour in rural areas for capital construction, such as road building and large water-construction projects. This process was supplemented by other forms of saving, e.g. through controls on wages and on prices of consumer goods, and the procurement programmes and taxation in the rural areas which enabled the government to restrain the consumption level and create budgetary surpluses to be used to import producers' goods and raise the level of capital formation. In Japan, during the early period of industrialisation based on imports of foreign capital and other resources, this latter policy of mobilising resources through high taxation was pursued as discussed in Chapter 2.

In China, budgetary surpluses were used for state investment as shown by the role played by basic construction investment by the government in total capital formation throughout the communist period. Tables 6.3 and 6.4 indicate the import content of capital investment in the production of machinery and equipment.

Table 6.3: Investment in Machinery and Equipment (in Millions of Yuan)

	Domestic Production	Net Imports	Total	From the USSR
1952	950	524	1,474	395.8
1953	1,234	733	1,967	389.9
1954	1,596	700	2,296	477.2
1955	2,081	746	2,827	535.8
1956	3,167	1,148	4,315	742.7
1957	2,765	1,189	3,954	652.7

Source: K. Chao, *Capital Formation in Mainland China, 1952-56* (University of California, 1974), p. 42.

Table 6.4: Import Content in the Total Supply of Certain Goods available to China 1953-6

	1953	1954	1955	1956
Metal-Cutting Tools	35.8	40.8	29.1	24.1
Forging Press Equipment	31.6	27.7	26.9	28.1
Rolled Steel	36.4	28.8	24.7	14.1
Non-ferrous Metals	38.2	34.2	11.9	8.2
Mineral Fertiliser	3.1	21.4	61.3	57.7
Soda Products	19.6	11.2	—	0.7

Source: A. Eckstein, *Communist China's Economic Growth and Foreign Trade* (McGraw Hill, 1966), p. 126.

According to another study, 50 per cent of Mainland China's machinery and equipment requirements for the first Five Year Plan had to be imported (Jen-Min-Jeh-Pao, *People's Daily*, 30 September 1957).

During the first Five Year Plan only 8.0 per cent of total equipment resources were allocated to agriculture.[30] At the same time agriculture is estimated to have carried the major burden of financing total investment.[31]

The official figures for food crop production alone show slower rates of increase, about 13 per cent for the first Five Year Plan.[32] When we consider these figures against the population increase of 11 to 12 per cent during the same period, the marginal rise in per capita consumption seems negligible. This situation raised the controversy over population growth amidst relative agricultural stagnation, as mentioned earlier. The Third World countries today are facing the same problem. But the official policies of these countries are laying more stress on controlling population, while China followed the policy of utilising the growing population through fundamental changes in economic organisation to stimulate capital formation. In the following section a survey of changes in agrarian organisation has been added, with their implications. The situation discussed above brought about a complete change in China's economic policy.

China felt the critical need to increase agricultural production, which could alone help her escape from the low-level equilibrium trap. But the Chinese leadership felt that this should be achieved through more productive use of labour because of its modest demand for the diversion of investment funds to agriculture. This could only be achieved if human resources were considered as the greatest capital asset. Hence the mass labour-mobilisation scheme leading to the formation of communes replacing collectives in 1958-9 clearly represents an attempt to find this kind of solution. This has been discussed in more detail earlier. It is to be noted here that primitive earth dams and partly constructed irrigation projects are not suitable when major floods or droughts occur as the developments of 1960 and 1961 showed. These were proved to be expensive and counter-productive. To mount the mass mobilisation schemes in such a way as to prevent the increases in production leading to increases in consumption, new institutional forms had to be devised. The small collectives of around 100 households were not suitable for this purpose; larger administrative and control units capable of managing huge integrated projects had to be developed. This new institutional reorganisation was meant to make more productive utilisation of available mass labour not only in agricultural production but also in developing manufacturing to supply inputs to farms as well as essential consumer goods. This was the essential role of communes. Thus the institution of communes entailed a much more far-reaching reorganisation of agricultural modes of production and institutions than the collectives did. Moreover, communes are more suitable to a labour-surplus economy than the collectives which are, on the other hand, more suitable to a labour-short socialist economy such as the USSR.

These institutional changes had a profound effect in terms of agricultural output as indicated by the fact that food crop production was around 205 million tons in 1958, which represents an approximate ten per cent increase as compared with 1955, as against a total rise of almost 25 per cent between 1952 and 1960.

In China agrarian reform policy has passed through a continuous process of change to make it suitable to meet the objectives of the industrial revolution. The following account demonstrates this role.

In China, agrarian reforms developed in three stages, i.e. (i) abolition of feudal land ownership; (ii) collectivisation based on the acceptance of the right to own private land; (iii) communes. The Agrarian Reform Law was introduced in China in June 1950.[33] The law described its aim as the abolition of the land ownership system of feudal exploitation, and called for the confiscation of landowners' land, draught animals, farm implements and surplus grain and for distribution to landless and land-hungry peasants. Under the law, the rural population was divided into five categories: landlords, rich peasants, middle peasants, poor peasants and workers, and farm labourers. The rich peasants and middle peasants were subdivided into different categories, depending on how much land they cultivated themselves and how much they rented out, the degree of exploitation, the number of farm labourers employed, and other considerations.

The most important change introduced by the new law was the exemption from confiscation of land belonging to rich peasants which was directly cultivated by them and their hired labour. It was also stated that land rented out by a rich peasant, except the amount he and his workers tilled, could be retained by its tenant. Even landlords were to keep their share of the redistributed land and if they owned industrial or commercial enterprises these too could be retained. Land cultivated by the owner and his own family was never to be drawn on for redistribution.

This measure obviously led to inequality in the distribution of land.

The Agrarian Law had the objective of establishing the principle of peasant proprietorship and not directly equalising the size of holdings. Article 1 of the law states categorically that 'the system of peasant land ownership shall be carried into effect'. This recognition of the principle of private property by a communist government was justified in Article 2 of the law which stated that the private ownership of land was intended to 'set free the rural productive forces, develop agricultural production and pave the way for the industrialisation in China'.[34]

This type of land reform could have adverse effects on production due to the uneconomic nature of redistributed lands. This is the experience of all underdeveloped countries today with respect to their land reform policy of redistribution of land ownership, unless accompanied by a positive policy of organising these units into large-scale productive units. In China, the reform law of 1950 has been criticised as having had an unfavourable effect on agricultural production. Under the law, land was taken away from those who were probably marginally the more efficient producers and given instead to those who were, if anything, less efficient. At the same time, though the average size of a holding can have been little different from before, there were more very small units of land than before. This situation is comparable to what is happening today in underdeveloped countries due to the negative nature of the land reform policy.

The government of China, however, recognised this negative character of land reform policy leading to the uneconomic nature of holdings and immediately introduced the policy of reorganising these into larger units in a positive step towards the formation of co-operatives, leading to collectivisation. But collectivisation in China was not successful due to the small size relative to the labour supply, and was replaced by communes. Communes were meant not only for agricultural development but also for industrial activities. In this way a successful process of industrial revolution evolved in China. This will be discussed in detail in the following section.

Recent Developments

The development policy until early 1960 was influenced by orthodox economic approaches, that is, while industrial development depended on agricultural development, rapid and sustained agricultural development ultimately depended upon industrial development, for the latter would contribute to the technical reform of the former through the provision of modern tractor-drawn machines, the introduction of chemical fertilisers and electrification, etc.

This is the strategy the present-day underdeveloped countries are pursuing with the basic difference that in China fundamental changes were made in the production relations in both the urban and rural sectors so that resources could be mobilised and more effectively utilised. But despite these organisational changes, the industrialisation policy, as stated above, failed to achieve an overall development.

Furthermore, China introduced a policy of socialisation of agriculture which in terms of its objective meant collectivisation as a condition for releasing resources for more effective utilisation. Abolition of serfdom and feudalism played this role in the classic case of the Industrial Revolution as well as in cases of imported industrialisation in nineteenth-century Europe and Japan. It is important to note here that underdeveloped countries in their development approaches in this respect are following the nineteenth-century practices of land reform with little success in achieving their objectives.

In the twentieth century the latecomer countries are already saddled with an acute problem of overpopulation in the agricultural sector with a limited modern sector based on imported capital and technology. It was true of pre-1917 Russia as well as of pre-1947 China. In these circumstances, the approach to land reform must be different from the one followed in the nineteenth-century industrialising countries because of the factor-endowment situation resulting from the pattern of investment pursued in these countries. The twentieth-century cases of industrial revolution, therefore, followed a land reform policy which in essence consists of three stages. The first stage is expropriation. Its purpose is to abolish the feudal institution of tenancy and to destroy politically the landlord class. The second stage is the redistribution of the expropriated land in equal holdings. Its purpose is to win the allegiance, support and participation of the agrarian masses and also to demonstrate the absurdity, under conditions of overpopulation, of distributing land in equal holdings on the principle of land for everyone. The third stage is the consolidation or collectivisation of the land, so distributed into sizeable areas under co-operatives or communes. It is in this final form that the reorganised agrarian structure is able to meet the challenge of the situation.

This strategy is an extension of what happened during the process of the first industrial revolution of the eighteenth century. Historical development since has called for this change.

This strategy can break through the vicious circle of poverty and rescue an overpopulated agricultural country from the conditions of overpopulation.

However, the limitations of the policy of collectivisation became evident soon. In Soviet Russia, collectivisation was only possible when preceded by a relatively sophisticated level of industrialisation capable of mechanising the countryside. But China's industry was incapable of supplying the machines and other products to make collectivisation work successfully. And the factor endowment situation in China was completely different from that of Soviet Russia. The supply of machines to agriculture without increasing its productivity would aggravate problems of rural unemployment. Russia, in its socialist approach towards the rapid growth of industrialisation, immediately faced a labour-shortage situation and therefore it appeared to be the proper course of action to collectivise agriculture with machinery to be supplied by industry, with a view to releasing both labour and food for industrialisation. In China, industrialisation based on imported capital was incapable of absorbing the rural population and, on the other hand, machines thus produced would have the effect of displacing rural workers. Mao Tse Tung wrote: 'In recent years capitalist spontaneity in the countryside has grown with each passing day . . . new peasants have sprung up everywhere, and . . . many well-to-do middle class peasants are striving to become rich peasants. On the other hand, many poor peasants lacking sufficient means of production are still living in poverty, some are in debt, others are selling or renting their land. If this tendency goes unchanged, the bipolar differentiation in the countryside will get worse day by day.'[35] This situation is comparable to the after-effects of the so-called land reforms followed in underdeveloped countries today.

The essential content of the agrarian reform was 'the confiscation of the land of the landlord class for redistribution to the landless or land poor peasants'. Thus the landlord class in society was abolished, and the land ownership system of feudal exploitation was transformed into a system of peasant land ownership.[36] This negative approach to land reform was followed by a positive one, i.e. collectivisation so that the effects of the land reform could be successfully utilised. The land reform could not solve the fundamental problems of small farmers. The fact that land holdings became more equal did not imply that farms were more viable. Indivisible items such as tools and draught animals could not be shared out equally, so that the new land divisions — which created more farms — exacerbated the shortage of such essential resources.[37]

To eliminate these problems and to establish a managerial structure to co-ordinate group activities, the policy of forming the co-operatives was initiated. Under the co-operative each peasant contributed his land to the co-operative as a 'share' and received annual dividend payments on it out of the profits as well as the normal remuneration for his labour. The peasant thus retained his right of private ownership, since his land represented a private investment in the co-operative. Farm animals and implements would be privately owned but collectively used during the early stages of a co-operative but after a period these would become collective property. Lastly, a fixed proportion of the annual yield of the co-operative was to be set aside for communal savings and welfare funds, the former for investment (to purchase equipment for the co-operative) and the latter for the welfare of poverty-stricken or disabled members.[38]

The economic case for co-operatives was associated directly with the advantages of a larger organisation in agriculture and unified management of the land. It would increase the available area through land consolidation, aid the introduction of more rational cropping patterns, and absorb surplus labour and the pool of unemployed by organising large-scale construction works which would otherwise be impossible under a system of small-scale fragmented agriculture. The building of reservoirs, irrigation channels, walls, dams and terracing would reduce the impact of natural calamities, thereby raising the productivity of the land and stimulating industrial development.

But the co-operative organisation, with private ownership of the means of production, created inefficiencies which hindered the growth of agricultural productivity. Ta Ung Ta-Lin wrote: 'Since the co-operative members still had their claim to private ownership of the land and other means of production, this inevitably placed restrictions on the rational use of the land, draught animals and farm tools. Furthermore, since it was necessary for co-operatives to distribute part of their farm produce to the members in the form of dividends on land and payment for other means of production, some members might more or less take advantage of the labour of the others.'[39] In other words, because of the organisational defects, resources that could be more effectively utilised were being misutilised. Therefore, the next step that was taken by the Chinese authorities was to establish collectives to eliminate the above limitations of co-operatives and thereby provide a greater potential for improvement in agricultural production. The collective 'converts the chief means of production owned privately by its members into collective property'. Peasants joining collectives were required to contribute their land, implements, tools and draught animals to the collective as shares and their values were paid in the form of collective shares or shares plus cash instalments to their owners.[40] The other features were the same as those of the co-operatives mentioned above.

However, this change of approach in the form of the elimination of private ownership and the establishment of a unified collective brought about a rethinking of the development approach in 1954. The pre-1954 approach was based on the idea that the development of agriculture is dependent on industrial progress, with the implication that collectivisation could not take place until the complete mechanisation of the country-side had been achieved. But under the new approach collectivisation was thought to be the pre-condition of mechanisation. This had been explained in a press release of the Ministry of Agriculture which states: 'Our ultimate aim is to mechanise agriculture completely on the base of . . . [collective] farming. This aim is achieved in two stages. The first involves concentration on organising individual peasants and creating the collect-ive ownership of the means of production in agriculture . . . In the second stage, the main emphasis will be on mechanisation which must depend on China's industrialisation.'[41] The form of economic development that was implied in this policy was that this institutional reform would per-mit technical advances which were largely independent of industry. Even without the existence of mechanisation, this institutional change was thought to be fundamental in mobilising the large pool of unemployed labour in the countryside. As we have noted in Chapter 2, the enclosure movement in Britain was not initially accompanied by mechanisation and thus did not release labour for industrial activities but helped by making more productive use of human resources in the country through large-scale organisation, and thereby introduced the technological changes in agriculture. In the former case though, it was planned and in the latter it was the result of private initiative due to two completely different historical situations.

In China, however, agricultural production did not show any encouraging trend, as indicated by grain production which rose by nine per cent and commercial crops which rose by ten per cent between 1952 and 1955, implying very little gain when it is considered against the pop-ulation increase during the period. This led to arguments in favour of birth control to curb an already existing labour surplus (economist Ma led this argument and generated Malthusian gloom that mechanisation before collectivisation would seriously aggravate the problem). In other words, the situation revived the controversy over collectivisation *vis-à-vis* mechanisation. According to those economists who advocated that mechanisation would have to precede collectivisation, a production ceiling had been reached that could only be broken through when the countryside had been provided with adequate assistance from industry in the form of tractors and other modern equipment. This argument had the flavour of the development strategy currently in vogue in under-developed countries. It became evident that the size of collectives already introduced on the Soviet pattern was not adequate for the vast population of China to generate technology suitable for the supply of labour, and on the other hand the surplus labour generated with the help of machines supplied by the industrial sector, which was based on Soviet capital and technology, could not be absorbed.

Mao Tse Tung advocated a more realistic approach suitable to China's factor endowment situation. According to him, the solution rested on the rapid and widespread establishment of co-operatives, followed by collectivisation which would lead to the extension of the agricultural unit to a size suitable to the factor supply situation, improve efficiency, make possible the more productive utilisation of labour resources, increase agricultural production and provide a greater surplus to industry, that would facilitate the industrialisation of agriculture. By combining the mobilisation of vast amounts of unemployed labour with the advantages of non-privately owned land, many urgent and practical improvements could be introduced to raise crop yields. These measures included the organisation of labour-intensive irrigation and soil conservation projects, the accumulation and application of natural fertilisers, the levelling and terracing of arable land, the protection and breeding of livestock, the use of superior seed strains etc.[42]

This approach of Mao preceded the formation of communes in China, the revolutionary economic organisation for industrial development suitable for an underdeveloped country with surplus labour. The role of population in China's development was stressed by Liu Shao Chi: 'It should be realised that machines are made and operated by men and materials are produced only through the efforts of men. It is man that counts; the subjective initiative of the masses is a mighty driving force.'[43] Liu's views followed what Mao said (as mentioned earlier).

This new approach known as the 'walking with two legs' policy gave top priority to heavy industry, but at the same time full attention was directed towards the development of agriculture and light industry. This is known as the policy of simultaneous development which was explained by Mao in February 1957: 'As China is a great agricultural country, with over eighty percent of its population in the villages, its industry and agriculture must be developed simultaneously.'[44] The accepted economic reasoning for giving priority to agriculture has achieved this policy, i.e. development will provide raw materials and a market for industry which will result in the accumulation of large funds for the building up of heavy industry. As light industry is closely related to agriculture, increase in the productivity of agriculture boosts light industry which in turn prepares the ground for heavy industry. The improvement in technology and modernisation requires more and more machinery, fertilisers, water conservancy, and electric power projects, and transport facilities for the former as well as fuel and building materials for the rural consumers. Thus greater growth in agriculture, inducing a correspondingly greater development of light industry, will stimulate the growth of heavy industry by providing demand for its products as well as funds for its development. In other words, industrial development in the natural course of history must be stimulated by the growth of indigenous forces originating from agriculture, agriculture being the largest sector with 80 per cent of the population depending on it.

It is also to be noted that to achieve this the organisation of production must change. Therefore it was realised that it was impossible to implement this new strategy on the basis of the collectives. A larger and more efficient form of organisation was required to ensure mobilisation of the vast amount of unemployed labour throughout the country to attain the above objectives without having any adverse effects on agricultural output. 'The peoples commune is characterised by its bigger size and more social-ist nature, with big membership and huge expanse of land the communes can carry out production and construction of a comprehensive nature and on a large scale. They not only carry out an all round management of agriculture, forestry, animal husbandry, side occupations and fishery but merge industry (the worker), agriculture (the peasant), exchange (the trader), culture and education (the student) and military affairs (militia men) into one.'[45]

Thus the commune is basically a self-sufficient multi-purpose unit responsible for the management of agricultural, industrial, commercial, cultural and military affairs within a given community. This organisation must have created enormous demand for labour. The commune was not only to mobilise labour for major public works in agriculture and to finance the development of local industry, but also to carry out such programmes as public security, health, education, banking, taxation and commerce. The economic objectives of the communes were to achieve a more efficient allocation of resources and to stimulate production. As part of the 'walking with two legs' policy, small-scale industries were established within each commune based on labour-intensive methods of production. The small enterprises had a number of advantages over their larger counterparts. They required less capital equipment and could more easily absorb funds from scattered sources; they required less time to con-struct and could produce more rapid results; they could be designed and equipped locally, and they could be established over a wider area thereby facilitating the completion of industrialisation throughout China.[46] This tremendous demand for labour for productive activities lies behind the self-sustained growth force in economic development.

To realise the full potential of the communes, the 'walking with two legs' policy proved to be a hindrance. From 1958 till early 1960 a severe economic crisis in the form of food shortages and fall in agricultural crop output necessitated a change in strategy. In the new strategy formulated in 1961 it was decided that successful economic development depended primarily upon a thriving and dynamic rural sector and that as a result top priority should therefore be given to the expansion of agricultural production. Thus the massive capital construction programme for heavy industry (obviously based on Soviet capital and technology) so consistently advocated during the period of the first Five Year Plan was to be cut drastically in 1961 so as to maximise the resources available for agricultural purposes.

The new strategy emphasised the need to develop the economy by concentrating upon agriculture, cutting back capital construction in heavy industry, reducing the urban population by transferring workers to the rural areas and changing the occupation of light and heavy industries so as to increase the output of consumer goods.[47] Under the 'walking with two legs' policy, emphasis on construction in the heavy industry sector created two problems, a shortage of labour to man various economic functions of the commune based on labour-intensive techniques on the one hand, and on the other hand a food shortage resulting from this inefficiency together with natural disaster in 1960.

Hence the new policy of treating agriculture as the foundation and industry as the leading sector states that the first importance is to be given to agriculture, and that the work of the industrial departments must be according to the policy of making agriculture the foundation of the national economy. Agriculture represented the foundation because without its stimulus, industrial development (e.g. rapid growth of heavy industry etc.) was impossible. In other words the type of heavy and modern capital goods industries China had been laying emphasis on before the 1960s must result from the increased productivity of the domestic resources, and therefore the process of industrial development should emanate from the need for, and as a result of, increased productivity in agriculture, as agriculture forms the basis of all pre-industrial economies and as such absorbs 80 per cent of the total population. Otherwise the development of heavy industries with the help of capital provided by foreign sources whether socialist or capitalist would create the type of problem China had faced before. The scale of industrial development is essentially dependent upon agriculture's capacity to expand production. Increase in the peasant's purchasing power, induced by agricultural development, would mean an ever expanding demand for finished industrial goods—producers' goods as well as consumer goods, which in turn would stimulate further industrial production. The development of agriculture would continue to centre round the commune as it was considered the best form of rural organisation for capital construction and the introduction and development of agricultural machinery to the countryside.[48]

With agriculture as the foundation, industry was given the role of the 'leading factor', which meant that industry was to divert resources into areas of production that would serve the agricultural sector, i.e. it would concentrate upon producing agricultural machinery, spare parts and repair equipment, chemical fertilisers, transport facilities, electricity, tools and building materials all of which would contribute to raising rural production. That is, the surplus created in agriculture was to be mobilised through reorganisation of the agrarian structure. This surplus would in turn be used to raise the productivity of the rural sector through technological improvement and thus a dynamic and self-sustained development process stimulating, and stimulated by, agricultural and industrial development would ensue. Because of the increased productivity under the commune a greater supply of consumer goods could be made available to the masses which would act as an incentive to increase productivity further.

Tables 6.5 and 6.6 show the effects of this policy on grain production and industrial production in China.

Table 6.5:   Estimated Grain Production in China, 1961-65 (in million tons)

Year	Jones (1)	Klatt (2)
1961	162	165
1962	174	180
1963	183	175
1964	200	190
1965	200	185

Sources: (1) E.L. Jones, *The Emerging Pattern of China's Economic Revolution, An Economic Profile of Mainland China* (Praeger, New York, 1968), p. 93.
(2) W. Klatt, 'Grain Production—Comment', *China Quarterly*, no. 35 (1968), p. 157.

The figures indicate a general trend of slow but steady improvement in grain production.

Industrial production shows the same trend as shown in Table 6.6:

Table 6.6: Estimated Production of China's Major Industrial Commodities, 1957-65

Product	1957	1958	1959	1960	1961	1962	1963	1964	1965
Electric Power (million kilowatt hours)	19	28	42	47	31	30	33	36	47
Coal (million tonnes)	131	230	290	270	180	180	190	200	240
Crude Oil (million tonnes)	1.5	2.3	3.7	4.5	4.5	5.3	5.9	7.0	10.0
Crude steel (million tonnes)	5.4	8.0	10.0	13.0	8.0	8.0	9.0	10.0	12.0
Chemical fertiliser (million tonnes)	0.8	1.4	2.0	2.5	1.4	2.1	3.0	3.6	5.5
Cement (million tonnes)	6.9	9.3	11.0	9.0	6.0	6.0	7.5	8.5	12.0
Timber (million cubic metres)	28	35	41	33	27	29	32	34	38
Paper (million tonnes)	1.2	1.6	1.7	1.7	1.0	1.0	1.1	1.5	1.8
Cotton Cloth (billion linear metres)	5.0	5.7	7.5	6.0	3.0	3.0	3.5	4.0	5.5
Sugar (million million tonnes)	0.9	0.9	1.1	0.9	0.7	0.5	0.5	1.1	1.6

Source: R.M. Field, 'Industrial Production in Communist China, 1957-65', *China Quarterly*, no. 42 (1970), p. 56.

The above discussion shows the basic pattern of the industrial revolution in a mid-twentieth-century overpopulated economy that resulted from socially conscious and planned (unlike the nineteenth-century ones) attempts to make more productive utilisation of domestic resources. Fundamental changes in economic organisation were needed to facilitate this process and thereby the development of technology. The most important lessons that we learn from China's history of trial and error is that (i) imported industrialisation cannot stimulate agriculture, even if the major sector of the economy is based on socialist principles; (ii) attempts at the simultaneous development of agriculture and industry in a socialist state with basic and heavy industries, where the main sources of increased productivity are based on foreign resources (even if these are provided by another socialist country) cannot be successful in achieving a self-sustained growth process; (iii) in the mid-twentieth century, a socially conscious and planned attempt requires reorganisation of the agrarian structure to release resources for more productive utilisation in order to stimulate indigenous technological development and thereby balanced industrial development.

Notes

1. W.A. Lewis, 'Economic Development with Unlimited Supplies of Labour', *The Manchester School* (May 1954); J. Fei and G. Ranis, *The Development of the Labour Surplus* (Homewood, Ill., 1964).

2. D. Jorgenson, 'Testing Alternative Theories of a Dual Economy' in I. Adelman and E. Thoerbecke (eds.), *The Theory and Design of Economic Development* (Johns Hopkins Press, 1966).

3. E. Domar, 'Capital Expansion Rate of Growth and Employment', *Econometrica*, no. 14 (1946), pp. 137-47; R.F. Harrod, 'An Essay in Dynamic Theory', *Economic Journal*, no. 49 (1939), pp. 14-33.

4. R.M. Solow, 'Technical Change and the Aggregate Production Function', *Review of Economics and Statistics*, no. 39 (1957), pp. 312-20.

5. H.J. Habakkuk, *American and British Technology in the Nineteenth Century* (CUP, 1962); N. Tranter, *Population since the Industrial Revolution* (Croom Helm, London, 1973), pp. 154-5.

6. R.M. Solow, 'Technological Progress, Capital Formation and Economic Growth', *American Economic Review*, no. 52 (1962), pp. 76-8.

7. J.L. Buck, *Land Utilisation in China* (University of Nanking, 1937), pp. 250-5.

8. Ibid., pp. 267-8.

9. T.J. Hughes and D.E.J. Luard, *The Economic Development of Communist China* (Oxford, 1959), p. 4.

10. J.L. Buck, *Chinese Farm Economy* (Chicago, 1930), p. 208.

11. Hughes and Luard, *Communist China*, pp. 5-6.

12. Ibid., pp. 6-7.

13. Buck, *Land Utilisation*, p. 9.

14. Hughes and Luard, *Communist China*, p. 7.

15. Ibid., p. 11.

16. A Chinese Government Information Handbook, *A China Manual* (1944), p. 126.

17. Ou Pao-San and Wang Foh Shen, 'Production and Employment in Pre-war China', *Economic Journal* (September 1946).

18. *A China Manual*, p. 126.

19. D. Mamo, 'Political Relations and Class Structure in Contemporary China', *International Symposium* (L'Bocconi University, 1976), pp. 16-18.

20. A. Eckstein, 'Sino-Soviet Economic Relations – A Reappraisal' in C.D. Cowan (ed.), *The Economic Development of China and Japan* (Allen and Unwin, London, 1964).

21. K. Chao, 'Policies and Performances in Industry' in A. Eckstein, W. Galenson and T.C. Liu (eds.), *Economic Trends in Communist China* (Edinburgh University Press, 1968), p. 570.

22. K. Chao, *Capital Formation in Mainland China, 1952-56* (University of California, 1974), p. 128.

23. Ma Yin-Chiu, 'My Philosophic Thoughts and Economic Theory', *New Construction* (November 1958), p. 142.

24. Ibid., p. 142.

25. Mao Tse Tung, 'Concerning the Correct Handling of the Contradiction among the People', 24 February 1957.

26. Ma, 'Philosophical Thoughts', p. 150.

27. Ibid., p. 151.

28. Chao, *Capital Formation*, p. 79.

29. K.C. Yeh, 'Capital Formation' in Eckstein, Galenson and Liu, p. 109.

30. A. Eckstein, 'The Strategies of Economic Development in Communist China', *American Economic Review* (May 1961), p. 509.

31. F.A. Mah, *The Financing of Investment in Mainland China* (Ramd., 1960).

32. H. Yin and Y. Yi, *Economic Statistics of Mainland China* (Cambridge, USA, 1960), p. 31.

33. *New China News Agency Supplement*, no. 54 (30 June 1950).

34. Ibid.; see also R.M. Breth, *Mao's China* (Longmans, London, 1976).

35. Mao Tse Tung, *On the Question of Agricultural Co-operation* (Foreign Languages Press, Peking, 1962), p. 27.

36. *The Agrarian Reform Law of the People's Republic of China* (Foreign Languages Press, Peking, 1959), p. 63.

37. K.R. Walker, 'Collectivisation in Retrospect: The Socialist High Tide of Autumn 1955–Spring 1956', *China Quarterly*, no. 26 (April/June, 1966), p. 4.

38. S.B. Thomas, 'Communist China's Agrarian Policy, 1954-6', *Pacific Affairs*, vol. 15, no. 2 (June 1956), p. 146.

39. Ta Ung Ta-Lin, *Agricultural Co-operation in China* (Foreign Languages Press, Peking), p. 57.

40. Ibid., p. 58.

41. *New China News Agency* (Survey of the Chinese Mainland Press, Peking, 20 Feb. 1955), no. 992, p. 35.

42. J. Gray, 'The Two Roads: Alternative Strategies of Social Change and Economic Growth in China' in S.R. Sacrum (ed.), *Authority, Participation and Cultural Change in China* (Cambridge University Press, 1973), pp. 119-20.

43. Liu Shao Chi, *Speeches in Second Session of the 8th National Congress of the Communist Party of China* (Foreign Languages Press, Peking, 1958), p. 49; Breth, *Mao's China*, p. 77.

44. Breth, *Mao's China*, p. 29.

45. R.R. Bowie and J.R. Fairbank, *Communist China, 1955-59* (Harvard University Press, 1965), p. 460.

46. Liu, *Speeches*, p. 49.

47. C. McDougall, 'The Road to Recovery', *Far Eastern Economic Review* (27 Sept. 1965), p. 586.

48. Breth, *Mao's China*, p. 77.

7 CONCLUSION

Economic development, being essentially a process of bringing about more productive utilisation of a country's human resources, needs as its basic condition the generation of indigenous technology which in turn necessitates fundamental changes in agrarian organisation. This technological change is induced by the increasing pressure of population on the existing technology and economic organisation. Agriculture, in the pre-industrial days, was the largest sector on which depended the entire fabric of social, political and economic life. Obviously, the pressure of population required technological change to meet the needs of the growing population which resulted in organisational change in agriculture to release resources to make this change a possibility. In this way, agrarian change culminated in the industrial revolution. This is the lesson we learn from both the classical industrial revolution of the nineteenth century and the two cases in the twentieth century. However, the former occurred spontaneously in a competitive *laissez faire* system, while the latter occurred in planned socialist systems.

In the nineteenth-century cases of successful development without an industrial revolution, we have noted that organisational change in agriculture led to the release of resources which were not, however, used to develop indigenous technology out of the rich heritage of pre-industrial technology but rather in Europe to import from the UK and in Japan from the other industrialised countries of Europe and the USA. The level of imported capital and technology at that time was, for obvious reasons, simple and labour-absorbing and hence, a process of dynamic and integrated development successfully evolved in these countries. In Japan, the integrated development process took a longer time to evolve which can be explained in terms of differences in the levels of technology of the mid-nineteenth and of the early twentieth centuries and in demographic changes of both periods.

In the mid-twentieth century, underdeveloped countries are attempting to bring about agrarian change through land reforms, but instead of developing indigenous technology of their own with resources released through such changes, they are depending on imported technology from labour-short, high-income countries which have different histories and factor endowments. Consequently, indigenous resources are lying idle and unproductive thereby perpetuating the problems of underdevelopment and of so-called overpopulation.

The prediction of Karl Marx that the introduction of Western capital into the colonial economies would result in the regeneration of these countries did not materialise. The main reason is that Western capital and technology have become increasingly labour-dispensing and have thus failed to create the hoped-for effects amongst the masses of population who are still living in a feudal, pre-industrial society. The important lesson to be learnt here is that technology must evolve through utilisation of indigenous resources which alone can create regeneration effects and thereby develop an indigenous culture.

APPENDIX: A NOTE ON INDIAN AGRICULTURAL SURPLUS AND THE INDUSTRIAL DEVELOPMENT — A HISTORICAL PERSPECTIVE

When the East India Company rule was established Indian agriculture could not be characterised as a subsistence peasant economy. This is, however, applicable to all economies of the world in their pre-industrial stages. This may be called a self-consumption stage which should be distinguished from a subsistence peasant economy. The former may be defined as producers consuming a part of their own produce and the latter as self-consumption by the peasants exhausting all the produce of the land. Both have their own rules and methods of transaction, own structure of crafts and own laws of production.[1] It is well known that India had a prosperous trading system and marketing network with flourishing handicrafts and cottage industries with their relatively advanced technology.[2] India had much larger and richer urban centres,[3] as discussed in earlier sections, with a much larger population depending on the non-agricultural sector at that time than it is today or during the colonial period. (See Chapter 3.) This urbanised social structure was based on surplus generated in the agricultural sector. Productivity in agriculture was also higher than in the West in pre-contact days as Slicher van Bath has shown. We have also noted in Chapter 3, following the analysis of Jones and Woolf, how this surplus was used by the ruling class and why this surplus did not culminate in an industrial revolution.

In a traditional system, land and labour being the only inputs, it was easy to locate the surplus land as being a free gift of nature and, labour being the only other factor, the excess produce over the cost of labour in real forms was the technical surplus. The Ruler's share of this produce was one third of the total produce or one quarter of irrigated land, the lower share being based on the argument that the producers had to put in extra efforts.[4]

The technical surplus was distributed among the rulers, intermediaries and producers. During the pre-colonial days this surplus was mostly used in the urban areas for conspicuous consumption, retaining the army, and for production of non-agricultural goods and services for kings and royal courts. The obvious question is what did happen to this surplus in the colonial period? How was the surplus in the hands of the state during the colonial period being used? What did the others do with the surplus in their hands?

The colonial administration abolished the traditional system of payment to the states in the form of a proportion of the total produce in kind and introduced in its place a system of fixed payment in cash in land revenue. In real terms the share of land revenue was estimated to vary between 6 to 20 per cent of gross produce depending on the nature of the soil and the availability of irrigation facilities.

Historically, land revenue was the main source of income to the East India Company which later on became the most important item in the budgets of the colonial government of India.

The following estimate of the share of the state in agricultural surplus during the colonial period is based on an unpublished paper by Dr Sipra Dasgupta.[5]

The Famine Commission of 1901 accepted ten rupees as the minimum expenditure for the survival of an average agricultural family for two months. Therefore, annual expenditure – the minimum just for survival – could be taken as £4.00 or 60 rupees.

Average holding at the time was six acres and the average value of crops was £1.00 per acre.

Hence:	Total Receipts	–	£6.00
	Simple Food Cost	–	£4.00
	Technical surplus	–	£2.00

Land revenue for a family was 45p at the rate of 7½p per acre. Hence land revenue covered 22.5 per cent of the 'surplus'. The rest was to take care of the family's expenditure on clothing, repairing huts and primitive tools, interest, local rates etc.[6]

Needless to say, very little of the state's share of the surplus flowed back for utilisation in agricultural or industrial development. For instance, the gross revenue of the Imperial Government was £19,300,000 in 1851-2 out of which £166,390 was spent on public works such as roads, canals, bridges etc.[7] No investment took place in other forms of capital inputs for agriculture, e.g. chemical fertilisers.

In India, the colonial government deliberately encouraged the export of traditional sources of manures like oil seeds and saltpetre which contributed handsomely to the favourable export trade balance. This favourable trade balance was used to finance the India Office superstructure in England and/or armed expeditions to the neighbouring countries. Such exports were considered extremely harmful to Indian agriculture. Dr J.A. Voelker, an agricultural chemist who was brought into India by the Imperial Government to advise steps to improve Indian agriculture wrote severely condemning such exports: 'We in England are not slow to avail ourselves of the advantages this export system offers and at the time of my leaving for India, I was feeding bullock at the Wiburn Experimental Farm on linseed cake and was growing crops with rape cake manure. Both materials, in all likelihood, were the produce of Indian soil and represented its transported fertility . . . a country which exports both crops and manure must be declining in fertility.'[8]

Industries that were introduced in India had seriously retarded economic development, as discussed earlier.

Today, surplus generated in the urban sector which, however, absorbs a much smaller proportion of total population than it did in the nineteenth century, is used for industrial development based on imported capital and technology with little indigenous labour-absorption effects. On the other hand, surplus generated in the agricultural sector is confined to a handful of large farmers who use expensive inputs either imported and/or produced in the country with foreign technology etc., and consequently such surplus in turn is used by this limited number of large farmers for consumption and investment. The large majority of peasants constitute the subsistence peasant economy. They have surplus in the form of disguised unemployment, food, shelter and clothing that go to their maintenance and therefore, it is not being used productively.

We have taken note of the existence of agricultural surplus which helped in the growth of relatively rich and large urban centres in India during the pre-contact days as well as during the period of the East India Company rule. The record also shows the evidence of developments of technology in pre-contact days which we noted earlier.

Under the circumstances, the failure of the long overdue transformation of agricultural techniques in India needs explanation. We have already mentioned that agricultural surplus was used for conspicuous consumption of the royal courts, landlords, native princes, merchants and bankers etc. during the Moghul period. During the colonial rule, the surplus was used to serve the interests of the rulers and, as seen, there was very little flow of this surplus back into the agricultural sector. Industries, however, were transplanted from abroad and had little effect on the demand for labour.

In the period after independence, although emphasis has been laid on rapid industrialisation, it has been essentially based on imported capital, technology and resources. We have earlier noted its impact on the economy.

Here we would like to discuss in brief the interrelationship between the transformation of agricultural techniques and the industrial development of a country.

It is well known that the long-overdue transformation of agricultural techniques in India was due to the absence of the industrial development of the country during the colonial period. The stimulus of growth in agricultural systems with well-established techniques, associated with an already given resource-structure—is a social, institutional set-up geared to the status quo and located outside agriculture—that is exogenous rather than endogenous to the system. The forces operating on both the demand and the supply side account for this.[9] Adam Smith wrote that, through the greater part of Europe, the commerce and manufacture of cities had been the cause and occasion of the improvement of the cultivation of the country.[10]

The urge to produce more than could be consumed by the producer's family depends largely on the growth of demand for agricultural products in the rest of the economy. This growth of demand was minimal during the colonial period and it has not been stimulated during the development decade. The demand here refers to the productive demand of the labour force in the non-agricultural sector. We know from the pattern of the sectoral distribution of the labour force that the proportion of the labour force engaged in the agricultural sector increased during the colonial period and now it has become stagnant at 75 per cent. Population growth during this period created demand for agricultural products, no doubt, but this growing demand unaccompanied by an increased productivity has resulted in the emergence and perpetuation of a subsistence peasant economy.

We noted before that the pressure of population demands technological change in agriculture which in turn necessitates organisational change to make resources available and organisation of production suitable for such technological changes to be effective. The technological change transforms the basically two-factor system (land and labour) of the 'empirical technique' into a three-factor system of land, labour and capital. The latter has varied forms, e.g. chemical fertilisers, insecticides, machines etc. The supply of these various types of capital when indigenously produced creates increasing demand for labour, food and other agricultural resources which stimulates technological innovation in agriculture and thereby industrial development. Thus the spread of scientific techniques raises the proportion of the purchased inputs in the total input structure of agriculture. The inputs of empirical techniques (i.e. techniques used in pre-industrial days) namely manures, seeds etc. are produced on the farm, whereas machines, improved tools, fertilisers etc. must come from the non-farm sector. In underdeveloped countries of today, these inputs are mostly based on foreign resources and technology which therefore have minimal demand for local resources. It is a well-known fact that the Green Revolution, which has been introduced in India to bring about changes in agricultural technology and practices requiring little organisational change, has failed to stimulate the economy.

Notes

1. H.W. Pearson, 'Trade and Market' in Polyani, Arensberg and Pearson (eds.), *The Early Empires* (Free Press, Glencoe, 1957), p. 323.

2. U. Dharampal, *Indian Science and Technology in the Eighteenth Century* (Impex India, 1971).

3. I. Habib, *The Agrarian System of Moghul India* (Asia Publishing, London, 1963), p. 76.

4. Irrigation was a traditional aspect of rural life in India. Hublee Canal, built by Emperor Shah Jahan in 1633, was already producing a net income of 76,000 rupees (£1,900) annually in the form of water rates to the ruler. See *The Report of the Royal Commission on Indian Agriculture* (1928), p. 325 and S. Dasgupta, 'The Relationships between Agricultural Growth and the Industrial Development – An Historical Perspective', an unpublished paper, Seminar on the Political Economy of Indian Agriculture, Calcutta, March 1973, p. 5.

5. Dasgupta, 'Agricultural Growth and Industrial Development'.

6. Ibid.

7. Karl Marx, 'Parliamentary Debate in India', *New York Daily Tribune*, 25 June 1853.

8. J.A. Voelker, *The Report on the Improvement of Indian Agriculture to the Government of India* (London, 1893), p. 106.

9. Dasgupta, p. 11.

10. Adam Smith, *Wealth of Nations*, Book III, Ch. XIV.

INDEX

Africa 53, 80, 85, 95, 98
agrarian structure, changes in 10, 15-
    16, 19, 20-1, 25-9, 39-41, 52, 54,
    111-12, 128, 135-6, 138-40, *see
    also* enclosures, land reform
agriculture, changes in 9, 14-16,
    17, 19-21, 56-8, 89, 105-7, 111-
    15, 124-6, 128, 132, 134, 138,
    140, 157, *see also* crop practices;
    mechanisation 19, 21-3, 28, 29,
    30, 34, 64, 116, 142, 144; product-
    ivity 14, 17, 19, 21, 22-3, 26, 28,
    29, 34, 36, 45, 51, 54, 57-8, 154;
    surplus 17, 22, 30, 32, 45, 56-7,
    154-8
aid, foreign 44, 74-5, 99, 135
Alcock, Michael 48
Allen, G.C. 55, 67n99, 68n111
Ashton, T.H. 33, 65n44
Asia 15, 53, 80, 98, *see also individual
    countries*
Australasia 92n44
Australia 11

Bairoch, P. 13n3, 17, 19, 20, 29, 45,
    64n3, 8-10, 12-16, 65n28, 66n75,
    72, 91n11
Baran, Paul 56, 68n106, 98-9, 101,
    103, 104n2, 11-13, 119n24
van Bath, B.H. Slicher 92n29, 154
bauxite 87
Belgium 42, 49, 73
Benedict, R. 80, 92n27
Blackwell 39
Boserup, E. 70, 90n1
Brazil 18, 85
Buck, J.L. 125, 150n7,10

Canada 11, 42, 92n44
capital, formation 17, 30, 45, 55, 56-
    7, 115, 118, 120, 123, 129-30,
    136-7; imported 9, 11, 14, 15-16,
    53, 54, 73, *see also* investment,
    foreign
Chambers, J.R.D. 33-4, 35, 65n46,49,
    66n52-3, 72, 90n3, 91n10
Chao, K. 133, 137, 151n21-2,28

Chile 18, 85
China 11, 14, 18, 21, 78, 80, 82,
    83, 89, 91n24, 117, Chap. 6
    passim; agrarian changes 21, 29,
    128-30, 135-6, 138-40, 141-3,
    144-5, 147-50; agriculture 124-5,
    128-9, 132, 134-5, 138-41, 143-
    9; and dualism 124, 128, 132-3;
    and investment 123-4, 127, 129,
    133, 136-7; and industrial trans-
    plantation 127-8; population 124,
    128, 135-6, 138, 144-5
Cipolla, C.M. 9, 12, 13n2, 11, 91n11,
    92n38,40
Clark, Colin 77, 91n22
Clough, S.B. 9, 13n9,28,39,40,41,47,
    65n22,28-9, 66n61,63
coal 22, 86
cocoa 84
coffee 85
Coke, Thomas 39
Cole, C.W. 28, 39, 65n25, 66n61
Cole, G.D.H. 33, 65n41
Cole, W.A. 26, 36, 65n32, 66n54
Collins, E.J.T. 23, 64n17, 66n70, 67n
    80
colonialism 12, Chapter 4 *passim*,
    110, 122, 153, 154-7
competition 10, 11, 62
copper 85
cottage industries 15, 24, 44, 126,
    154, *see also* handicrafts
cotton 22, 48, 84, 86
Crawcour, E.S. 52, 67n91
crop practices 16, 17, 19, 21, 22, 27,
    29, 30, 35, 38-9, 58, 83, *see also*
    agriculture

Dasgupta, Sipra 155, 158n5
Deane, P. 26, 36, 65n32, 66n54
Denmark 30, 42, 106, 125
depopulation 94
development, theories of 9, 18-19,
    see also underdevelopment
Dobb, M. 105, 107, 108, 111, 113,
    115, 117, 118n1-7,10-14,20,
    119n25,29

159